SIKHS AND THEIR WAY OF LIFE

It is a pleasure to commend this book in its reprinted format, particularly knowing the Author and respecting his work and service to teachers. He is an educationalist himself, and as such, enables them to understand and respect the Sikh faith and way of life.

The style is succinct and direct, enabling the reader to grasp quickly the information they seek. It will benefit the busy teacher and senior student alike. They may have confidence in its accuracy knowing that Gurinder Singh Sacha is a practising Sikh and an honoured member of his community.

Ronald H Aldrich BD. BTh. F.R.G.S.
Adviser Religious Education
London Borough of Redbridge

THE SECOND EDITION

I feel pleased to be able to revise and add substantially to this second edition of 'The Sikhs and their way of life'. The major additions include —

i)   Political and social background of the Sikhs;
ii)   Sikh symbols and the law;
iii) Panjabi Language and script;
iv)   the Akal Takhat and the Harmander
v)   extracts from the REHAT MAYADA

I hope that the readers will accept this book as my very humble contribution towards promoting better understanding about the Sikhs and Sikhism.

G.S. Sacha
November 1987

LIST OF MAPS, PICTURES AND OTHER SKETCHES

THE SIKHS AND THEIR WAY OF LIFE

CONTENTS   PAGE

AUTHOR'S NOTE

It is often said that ignorance is a cause of fear and prejudice. This leads to many inequalities and intolerant behaviour by one person to another and by one group of people to another. Therefore, the remedy lies in reversing the process. Only true knowledge can dispel ignorance and fear and the resultant understanding will contribute towards peace and harmony among people. But this is easier said than achieved.

Now, this humble contribution 'THE SIKHS and THEIR WAY OF LIFE' is one other drop in the ocean of knowledge which already exists. However, this book can be particularly useful to two groups of people.

(a) **The Teachers of Multicultural Studies.** Those who neither have any direct experience of the Sikh Faith nor could find enough suitable materials about the Sikhs for their classroom use. They are neither specialists in religious education nor can they afford to spend too much of their time studying detailed descriptions of the history and beliefs of every faith or ethnic group. For them, this book endeavours to cover the maximum number of aspects of the Sikh people with the minimum number of words. It is hoped that a couple of hours of conscientious reading of this book would provide them with much of the relevant information which they would need to know before passing it on to their pupils.

(b) **The Sikh Children.** Those who are born and brought up away from the 'homeland' of the Sikhs and, as such, have little or no opportunity to acquire naturally the history, as well as the cultural and religious standards, of the 'SIKH FAITH'. These are the children whose parents are (i) either too busy to tell them enough about the teachings and traditions of their own religion, or (ii) are too shy to explain to their children because of their certain personal weaknesses and other limitations such as the confident use of each other's first language i.e. Panjabi and English. To such SIKH children this book would serve as an important formal 'introduction' and would, hopefully, generate in them further interest to know more about their own religion.

Gurinder Singh Sacha
January 1983

77 Jarrow Road
Chadwell Heath
Romford, Essex

FOREWORD

Sikhism is a religion of divinity within a human framework, protest (against injustice) and brotherhood of man. Implicit within its precept is a conscious and continuous process of struggle against oppression, and affirmation of traditional values deeply rooted in the hearts of the people of Panjab — the land of the five rivers. Sikhism was not only a revolt against the Brahminical Caste structure, but also the beginning of a political uprising against Islamic domination and persecution. Guru Nanak laid the foundation of a long ideological war of liberation fought consistently over the lives of the Gurus on: "the doctrine that the lowest is equal to the highest, in race, as in creed, in political rights, as in religious hopes".

It was a Grand Design, and it was left to Guru Gobind to grasp the full spiritual, political, social and cultural implications and to activate the ideology, and give it form, substance, structure and force to complete the process . . "Nanak's God loved his Saints; Gobind's God destroyed his enemies. The sacramental ceremony for the baptism of the 'panj piyara' (five beloved ones) which is a symbolic rite was introduced by Guru Gobind on the auspicious Baisakhi (new year) in 1699, and acted as the catalyst that dramatically redefined Sikhism. Out of this historical event emerged a new 'community', a new 'congregation', called the 'Khalsa' which became the armed political wing of Sikhism. This created a lasting tradition of militancy and protest against social injustice, oppression and inequality. The Khalsa acquired the symbolic collective and individual identity with the five K's as a marker of the 'panth' — reflecting and representing the ideology of Sikhism.

This book goes a long way to explain the global core of a world religion, and in my view the only way to interpret the contents of this book is that Sikhism stands for divinity, brotherhood and protest. Any other interpretation would invalidate the core of a world faith.

Tuku Mukherjee
February, 1983

Southlands College
Roehampton Institute, (LONDON)

BACKGROUND INFORMATION

The homeland of the SIKHS is the PANJAB state in INDIA and so PANJABI is the language of the SIKHS.

There are about 12-13 million Sikhs; at least 9 million living in the state of PANJAB, the rest well dispersed in many other states of Northern India and in big cities like Delhi, Calcutta and Bombay.

Sikhs are well-known for their spirit and adventure, and many have travelled abroad, settling in East Africa, Malaysia, Singapore, Britain (South-east and Midlands), Canada (Ontario and British Columbia) and U.S.A. (California).

Although the Sikhs are less than 2% of the total Indian population, their influence has been felt in most aspects of Indian life. Some of their most outstanding contributions are in the field of:—

FARMING
Because of the enterprising nature of the Sikhs, Panjab leads the rest of India in the use of modern farm machinery. Sikh farmers are highly efficient, and using modern methods they have produced record yields for crops such as wheat, sugar-cane, rice and cotton.

THE ARMED FORCES
Sikhs are renowned for their martial spirit. Inthe past, and especially during the first and second world wars, there was hardly a Sikh family whose son or other male relative had not joined the Army. No wonder that within India the highest number of 'battle honours' were awarded to the Sikhs.

TRANSPORT AND INDUSTRY
Throughout northern India and in the larger cities like Calcutta, Delhi and Bombay, the road transport industry seems to be dominated by the Sikhs, many of whom own fleets of trucks and taxis. Similarly, Sikhs have earned a reputation as a skilled workforce in the Indian iron and steel and machine tool industries.

EDUCATION AND SPORTS
In the field of Education, the Panjab State of India was not among the leaders in the past, but there are now four Universities, one each at Amritsar, Ludhiana, Patiala and Chandigarh. Moreover, education is free and compulsory up to the age of 14.

The Sikhs are some of India's finest sportsmen. They excel, especially, in hockey, wrestling and athletics.

POLITICAL FREEDOM
The Sikhs have always participated enthusiastically in political affairs at both local and national level. During the Indian Independence movement, Sikh volunteers were constantly at odds with the 'Raj' authorities as they often spearheaded the non-violent struggle for freedom led by Mahatma Gandhi. For example —
>   of the 121 Indian freedom fighters who were hanged for their Anti-Raj activities, 93 were Sikhs;
>   of the 2646 Indians who were given life imprisonment for their Anti-Raj actions 2147 were Sikhs;
>   of the 1302 who died as a result of General Dyer's 'shoot to kill' orders 799 were Sikhs. (This shooting incident happened on the Baisakhi day of 13th April 1919 at Jallian Wala Bag in Amritsar, and ever since it is remembered as Jallian Wala Bag Massacre.)

Similarly, during the so-called 'emergency' in 1976 when the then Prime Minister of India, Mrs. Indra Gandhi, dissolved the democratically-elected parliament and assumed autocratic powers to rule the country, the Sikhs were the most noticeable opposition who continued their voluntary arrests in thousands each week in the course of protesting against the law publicly and peacefully until democracy was restored in 1978.

Indeed, Guru Nanak, the founder of the Sikh faith, had himself set the pace for freedom and justice by commenting critically on the contemporary political and social situation in India, and by protesting publicly against the injustice and tyranny practised by the Mughal Emperor Baber — for which he was charged by the state and imprisoned with hard labour.

However, since the independence of India in 1947, Sikhs have learnt with bitterness that they have been betrayed by those political leaders in whom they had placed their trust. Although historically Sikhs have always responded effectively to any direct threats to their existence, in recent years they have become extremely vulnerable to the cruel onslaught of the biased media which are almost entirely controlled by the majority community of India.

One needs to understand that because of their past history and record of valour in war, the Sikhs are often described as a martial race. This does not mean that the Sikhs are prone to violence. Any such action is approved only if taken as a last resort in self defence and to uphold righteousness. Guru Gobind Singh put it in these words —

"When all other means of righting evil fail, it is legitimate to use the sword".

This thinking is very close to the United Nations' Universal Declaration on Human Rights —

"WHEREAS IT IS ESSENTIAL IF MAN IS NOT TO BE COMPELLED TO HAVE RECOURSE, AS A LAST RESORT, TO REBELLION AGAINST TYRANNY AND OPPRESSION, THAT HUMAN RIGHTS SHOULD BE PROTECTED BY THE RULE OF LAW".

SOCIAL BEHAVIOUR

The religion of the Sikhs forbids them to believe in the caste system. However, not all Sikhs have been able to dissociate themselves fully from this unnecessary practice which is the legacy of Hinduism.

Again, although many Sikhs still regard themselves as belonging to certain groups or castes, such as Aroras, Bhataras, Jats, Khataris, Ramgharias, Sainis etc, these divisions should not be seen as divisions representing higher or lower castes.

Also, we need to remember that just as, in almost every major religion, there exist certain groups or sects which seem to be practising or preaching slightly differently from the 'main body', similarly such sects appear also in the Sikh community although their number remains very insignificant.

Sikhs usually marry within their own religion, but allowances are made when a partner from an outside faith shows interest and willingness to accept the Sikh way of life. Similarly, there are examples when a Sikh boy or a girl has not felt obliged to remain a Sikh by marrying a non-Sikh — to the distress of parents and relatives. However, such cases are very few and are in line with other faiths.

In present-day Panjab (Sikh homeland), early or child marriage is forbidden by law. A girl may not marry before she is 18 and the minimum age for the boy is 20. Both widows and widowers can remarry.

Sikh women enjoy a much greater degree of equality of opportunity in all spheres of life than their counterparts in many other communities. For example, Sikh women can often be seen reading and reciting the holy scriptures to the congregation in a Gurdwara, or taking an active and sometimes leading role on occasions such as political conferences, protest marches and rallies in support of their community.

Interestingly, no ARDAS (Sikh congregational prayer) is complete without remembering the extraordinary role of the Sikh woman in terms of their sufferings and sacrifices in the making of Sikh history.

Sikhs are renowned for their warm hospitality, and for their spirit of sharing and sacrifice. Strangers and members of other faiths are always welcome to visit a Gurdwara as long as they observe some simple rules, for example removing shoes and covering the head before entering the holy room or the hall. Similarly, tobacco and alcohol are strictly forbidden inside the Gurdwara premises.

Again, most Sikhs would not be very happy if a visitor started smoking inside their house — although they may give a totally opposite impression, out of hospitality, by being courteous to the innocent offender. Although forbidden in Sikh scriptures, not every Sikh has been successful in resisting western influence in the use of alcohol at some public or private gatherings.

The Government and the people of KENYA honour Sikh insignia KHANDA on the occasion of 4th World Conference on Unity and Peace held in August 1984 by issuing a new postage stamp.

4th World Conference AUGUST 23-31 1984
KENYA 3·50

"THE BRAVE SIKHS OF PANJAB ARE ENTITLED TO SPECIAL CONSIDERATION. I SEE NOTHING WRONG IN AN AREA AND A SET-UP IN THE NORTH WHERE THE SIKHS CAN ALSO EXPERIENCE THE GLOW OF FREEDOM".

MR. JAWAHAR LAL NEHRU:
the first Prime Minister of India, father of Mrs. Indira Gandhi and grandfather of Mr. Rajiv Gandhi.

On the occasion of the session of All India Congress Committee at Calcutta on 6th July 1946 and as reported in the Statesman, 7 July 1946.

"I ASK YOU TO ACCEPT MY WORD AND THE RESOLUTION OF THE CONGRESS THAT IT WILL NOT BETRAY A SINGLE (SIKH) INDIVIDUAL MUCH LESS A COMMUNITY . . . LET GOD BE THE WITNESS OF THE BOND THAT BINDS ME AND THE CONGRESS TO YOU".

MAHATMA GANDHI:
While speaking to a Sikh congregation at GURDWARA SISGANJ in Delhi and further assuring their position in case of betrayal by the Congress Government in the future.

"THE SIKHS COULD IN THAT CASE TAKE THEIR KIRPANS IN HAND WITH PERFECT JUSTIFICATION BEFORE GOD AND MAN".

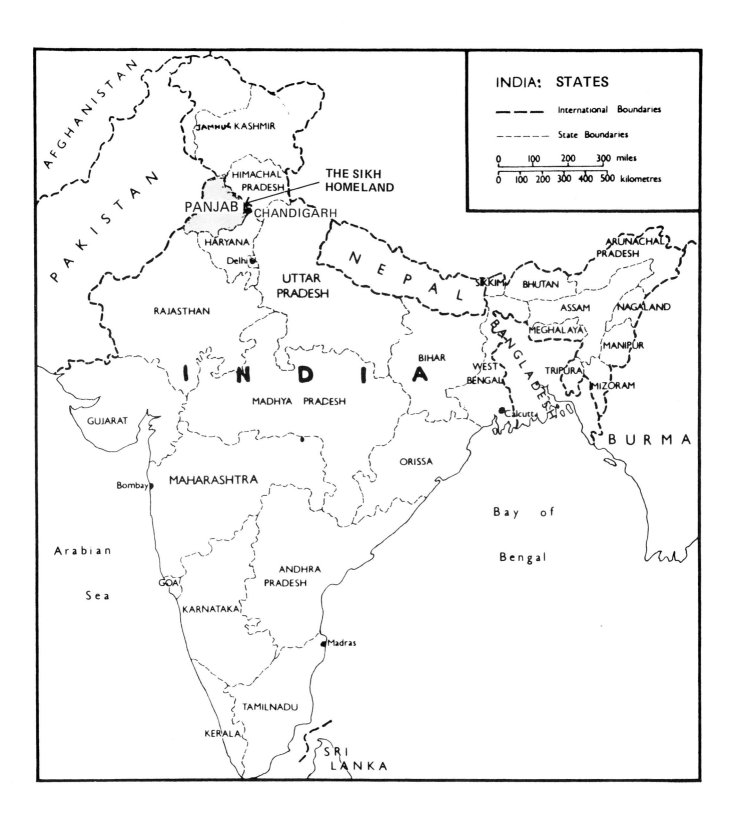

STATES with 10,000 or more SIKHS (figures rounded up to the nearest thousand)

ANDHRA	13,000	J. & KASHMIR	110,000	U.P.	400,000
ASSAM	12,000	M. PARDESH	100,000	W. BENGAL	36,000
BIHAR	62,000	MAHARASHTRA	104,000	DELHI	300,000
GUJRAT	19,000	ORISSA	11,000	CHANDIGARH	70,000
HARYANA	650,000	PANJAB	9,000,000		
HIMACHAL	48,000	RAJASTHAN	350,000		

GURU NANAK
(1469—1539)

"Among the low let my caste be the meanest,
Of the lowly, let me the lowliest be.
O Nanak! let such be the men I know,
With such men let me keep company.
Why should I try to emulate the great?
Where the fallen have protected been
is your grade and your goodness seen."

Guru Nanak

GURU NANAK

Guru Nanak, the founder of Sikhism, was born in 1469 in a small village (TALWANDI) near LAHORE in PANJAB. The place is now called NANKANA SAHIB and is in Pakistan.

NANAK was a Hindu by birth, but he soon revolted against the religious trappings, paraphernalia and the caste-system of Hinduism.

He was equally unhappy about the way some Muslim preachers or Mullahs preached intolerance and fanaticism in the name of religion, which often led to bloodshed, tyranny and oppression of those who did not accept Islam.

He declared himself as belonging to neither Hindus nor Muslims but the whole human race.

At the age of thirty, Guru Nanak thus started on his 'great journeys' on foot to convey 'HIS MESSAGE' from village to village, town to town in the true traditions of the 'great men' before him, just as Buddha had done, as Christ had discoursed, as Mohammed had proclaimed.

Nanak always stressed that he was a mere servant of God, and that he was only concerned with doing 'GOD'S WILL' in the world.

In his preachings Guru Nanak suggested practical ways of countering selfishness, ignorance and all that is evil. The spiritual and social welfare of the common people was his prime concern.

According to Nanak the political and cultural domination of the people by the ruling and priestly classes was chiefly responsible for their degeneration and degradation. He gave these demoralised people a new conscious-ness which was based on the principle of the 'unity' and 'fatherhood' of God and the equality and brotherhood of man.

Guru Nanak's teachings were a direct challenge to the authority of the priestly class and the inhumanity of the ruling tyrants, and there were times when he was ridiculed, stoned and even imprisoned. But Nanak was never afraid to raise his clear voice against cruelty, injustice and falsehood.

The people to whom Guru Nanak talked and preached found something special and different from what they already knew; and those who followed him or his preachings closely, came to be known as SIKHS meaning learners or followers. Both Hindus and Muslims were among Guru Nanak's followers.

These followers of Sikhs called him the true Guru (prophet). He was truly the prophet of the people. He lived amongst them, shared their joys and sorrows and taught them the way of honest and truthful living. He always stressed this to his followers by saying

"Truth is high. But higher still is truthful living."

He died in 1539.

"Not the ascetic way,
But a life of truth and love
Amid the world's temptations,
Is the secret of spiritual life.

Put away thy pride.
The essence of religion is humility,
Service, sympathy.
Not the yogi's garb and ashes,
Not the shaven head,
Not long prayers,
Not recitations and torturings. . ."

Guru Nanak

THE FOUR GREAT JOURNEYS OF GURU NANAK

Guru Nanak's life of 70 years can be divided into three parts.

The first 30 years he spent at home where he grew up as a 'mystery' child, was married, took up employment, but was always seen behaving differently from the ordinary householder.

The next 22 years he spent travelling in India and abroad 'on God's call' and taking up the task of spreading Truth and Love wherever he went.

For the last 18 years he settled down back in the Panjab at KARTAR PUR (now in Pakistan) living among his followers and inspiring them to a life of honest and truthful living.

THE DIVINE CALL

From the birth of Guru Nanak till his death his life is full of mystery stories about him. One such story marks the beginning of his four great journeys which took him 22 years to complete.

One day, when Nanak was about 30 years old, he went to the VAYEN NADI (a nearby river) to bathe and meditate as usual. But this time, as he dipped his head under the water, he did not come out. Some people noticed his clothes were left on the bank and became very concerned. No one could establish Nanak's whereabouts; most thought that he had been carried away by a strong current and was probably dead. However, some started a twenty-four-hour vigil as they had complete faith that Nanak was alive, and faith in his mysterious ways.

Two nights had passed. On the third day, to the pleasure and amazement of some people near the river, Nanak was seen walking out of the water at the same spot where he had disappeared two days earlier. Soon the people gathered around him and asked questions. He only pointed his finger to the skies and remained silent. This did not stop the crowd getting bigger and questions getting harsher.

At last he spoke: "I have received a call from the AKAL PURKH (The Timeless God). He has favoured me with a task to go and spread 'His message' to all people far and near. God does not belong to Hindus or Muslims alone. He considers all people alike and equal. The distinction between Hindu and Muslim is false. This is true, and this is His message."

There were more questions. In the end, everyone present including the chief Qazi was amazed at what he said and was further convinced that Nanak was a divine being.

After this, Nanak resigned from his job as store-keeper and made plans to embark on his 1st great journey to the East. Two of his followers and friends showed their desire to go with him; Nanak was even more pleased to have their company. One was Baala; he was a Hindu by birth, the other was Mardaana and he was a Muslim. Wherever the Guru went, they went with him.

Guru Nanak's 1st journey lasted for about 10 years (1500-1510). He went eastwards via HARDWAR to as far as ASSAM and then turned homeward through BENGAL, ORRISA visiting another holy place of the Hindus called PURI.

Guru Nanak's 2nd journey lasted for about 4 years (1510-14). This time he travelled southward reaching SANGLADEEP or SRILANKA, and then returning roughly along the west coast through Kerala, Gujrat and Sindh.

Guru Nanak's 3rd journey took him to the north and lasted for about 2 years (1514-16). He visited places far beyond KASHMIR which included parts of the present USSR and TIBET.

Guru Nanak's 4th journey was the last and the longest and lasted for about five years (1517-22). This time he travelled west. He visited the holy places of the Muslims, MAKKAH and MADEENA, and then travelled through BAGDAD, TEHRAN, MASHAD, and KABUL before returning to the Panjab.

"As fragrance dwells in a flower,
And reflection in a mirror,
So does God dwell in every soul;
Seek him therefore, in thy self."

Guru Nanak

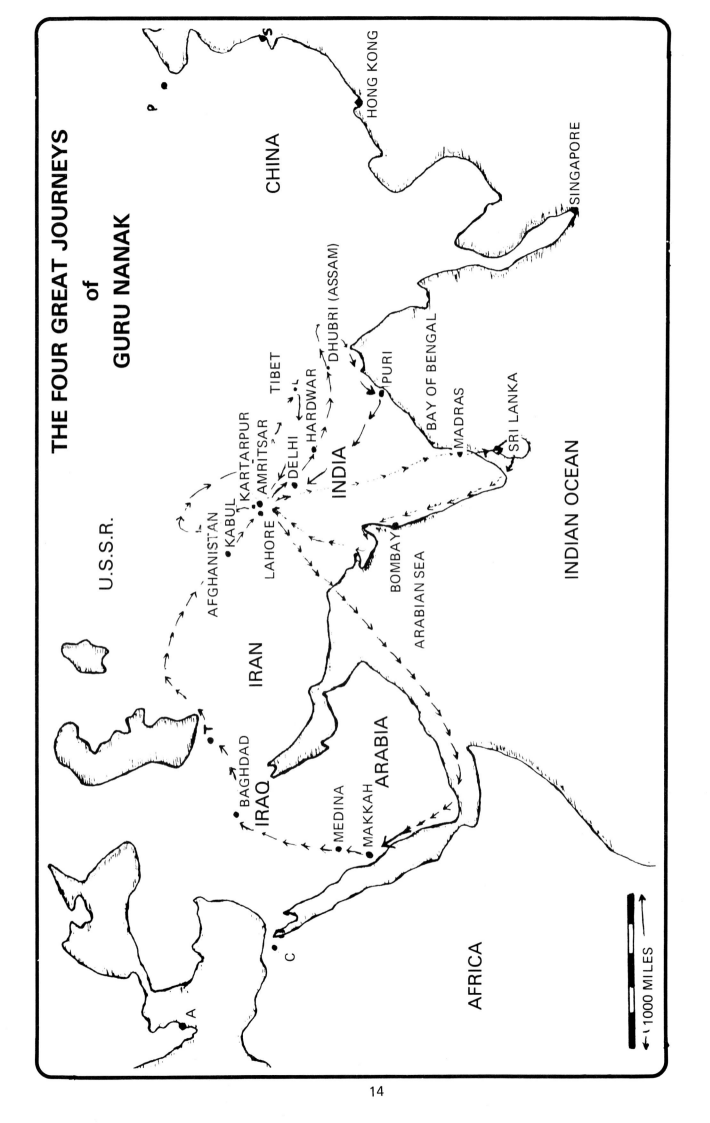

THE FOUR GREAT JOURNEYS
of
GURU NANAK

GURU GOBIND SINGH

(1666–1708)

"I will make sparrows hunt down hawks;
I will turn jackals into fierce lions;
And make one single Sikh fight a legion."

"The Khalsa is my own form;
I manifest myself through the Khalsa.
So long as Khalsa remains distinct;
I bestow all glory on them."

Guru Gobind Singh

AFTER GURU NANAK

Guru Nanak's message was carried forward to his nine successors. Their names are:

GURU ANGAD (1504 - 52) — Popularised Panjabi language and script.

GURU AMARDAS (1479 - 1574) — 'Outlawed' 'Pardah' and 'Satti' among Sikhs.

GURU RAMDAS (1534 - 81) — Founded the present city of AMRITSAR.

GURU ARJAN (1563 - 1606) — Compiled 'Adi Granth', the first 'Martyr Guru'.*1

GURU HARGOBIND (1595 - 1644) — Introduced two swords of 'Meeri' and 'Peeri'.*2

GURU HAR-RAI (1630 - 61) — 'The promoter of the Sikh Faith.'

GURU HAR-KISHAN (1656 - 64) — 'The Child Guru.'

GURU TEG-BAHADUR (1621 - 75) — 'The protector of the Hindu Faith'; the second 'Martyr Guru'.*3

GURU GOBIND SINGH (1666 - 1708) — 'The Founder of the Khalsa'; the Saint and Soldier.

---

*1 The First Martyr Guru — The great Mogul Emperor Akbar was a kind and tolerant ruler. When he died in 1606, he was succeeded by his son Jahangeer, whose attitude towards Sikhs was much different. Soon he found an excuse to punish Guru Arjan because even some Muslims were attracted to his teachings. The Emperor Jahangeer himself wrote in his memoirs — "I issued orders that he should be converted to Islam, or be imprisoned, tortured and executed under some political pretext." Thus on May 30th, 1606 Guru Arjan was summoned to the King's court to explain his conduct. Then, after some questioning he was made to sit on a red hot iron plate while burning sand was poured over from the top. He was thus tortured to death when he was made to bathe in the Ravi river, immediately after.

*2 'Meeri' stands for temporal power and 'Peeri' for spiritual authority.

*3 The Second Martyr Guru —The year was 1675. This was the time when Aurangzeb was the emperor at Delhi. He was a fanatic and deeply committed to the promotion of Islam even by forcible conversions. When some Hindu Brahmans from Kashmir approached the Guru Teg Bahadur to intervene, he went to Delhi to discuss the matter with the emperor. But the emperor, rather than listening to the Guru's pleading, gave him two choices —either to accept Islam or face death. He was publicly beheaded in an open square called Chandni Chowk in Delhi. Now, a magnificent Gurdwara called 'SEES-GANJ' stands at this historic square where the Guru gave his life so that a nation could live.

A few miles away close to the Parliament House in New Delhi stands another proud landmark of the Sikhs, a Gurdwara called 'Rikaab Ganj' where the Guru's body was cremated.

"Nanak preached the gospel of peace; but there was no peace for Sikhs in the empire of the Mughals. Just as the Romans sought, by unremitting persecution, to stamp out Christianity, so the Mughal Emperors sought to stamp out The Khalsa. Like the Romans, they succeeded only in strengthening that which it was their purpose to destroy."

C. H. Payne

GURU GRANTH SAHIB JI

Before his death Guru Gobind Singh, the 10th Guru, ordained that from then on 'Adi Granth' should be recognised as the manifest body of the Gurus — and hence the name Guru Granth Sahib Ji.

The Guru Granth is the 'Holy Book' or the Sacred Scriptures of the Sikhs. No Sikh ceremony is regarded as complete unless it is performed in the presence of the Holy Granth.

The Granth is written in Panjabi and contains the actual words and verses as uttered by the Sikh Gurus. It was first compiled by Guru Arjan **in 1604** and then added to and recopied by the 10th Guru Gobind Singh. Every copy of the Holy Granth, whatever the size, must consist of **1430 pages.** A unique feature of the Granth is that it also contains a good number of passages of verses written by non Sikh Saints i.e. Muslims, Hindus and even so called 'untouchables'. This was done to demonstrate the Sikh's respect for other saints and tolerance for all faiths. Altogether the Granth includes **5,894 SHABADS** (hymns or holy verses) which are arranged in **31 RAGAS** (musical measures).

The Holy Granth is given the utmost respect by the Sikhs and is accorded the same reverence as would have been given to the Living Prophet. In the Gurdwara it is placed on a dais with a canopy above and is covered with the best available and often richly embroidered cloths or materials. Sikhs usually place an offering in cash or kind or both as they approach the Holy Granth, and bow down low on their knees to show their respect. A 'Granthi' (one who reads the Granth) or a sewadar (volunteer) remains in constant attendance and holds a **CHOWR** (a symbolic whisk of sovereignty) which he occasionally moves over the 'Holy Book.'

The first correct English version (translation) of the Granth was made by Max Arthur Macauliffe and was published by Oxford University Press in 1909. But before Macauliffe, a German missionary, Dr. Ernest Trumpp, had also attempted to translate the Granth into English in 1877, which was later considered as poor and untrustworthy by the Sikhs. However, another rendering of the Granth, and in free verse, is done by Dr. Gopal Singh, although Dr. Manmohan Singh has also produced an excellent translation in free verse.

Extracts from comments by some non Sikh eminent scholars of comparative religion —

1. **Duncan Greenless** (Christian)
"the Guru Granth Sahib is certainly one of the world's masterpieces of poetry. It is legitimately the 'Bible of the Universal Religion' ".

2. **Professor Abdul Majid Khan** (Muslim)
"In the real sense of the word, the Guru Granth is a synthesis of scriptures, a spiritual dictionary and a marvellous book, meant for the betterment and spiritual uplift of humanity."

3. **Dr. Rajindera Parasad** (Hindu)
"The Sikh Gurus were patriots and reformers, but in no way partisans. What is more they believed in practising TRUTH rather than merely preaching it. The Adi Granth is indeed a monument to their universal and rational outlook, their catholicity and earnest search for spiritual truth."

4. **Miss Pearl S. Buck**
"Shri Guru Granth Sahib is a source-book, an expression of man's loneliness, his aspirations, his longings, his cry to God and his hunger for communications with that Being. I have studied the scriptures of other great religions, but I do not find elsewhere the same power of appeal to the heart and mind as I find here in these volumes."

5. **Prof. Arnold Toynbee**
'.... The Adi Granth is part of mankind's common spiritual treasure. In this coming religious debate, the Sikh religion and its scriptures, the Adi Granth will have something of special value to say to the rest of the world .... For Nanak, the fundamental truth was that, for a human being, the approach to God lies through self-abnegation.

SIRI GURU GRANTH SAHIB JI

THE STORY OF THE BIRTH OF KHALSA

It was the BAISAIKHI day. The year was 1699. As usual Sikhs from far and near had gathered together at ANANDPUR to celebrate the New Year Festival. However, the gathering was a bit different that day. This year GURU GOBIND RAI had sent a message that every Sikh who could afford to come, must come to the annual fair. They should come to ANANDPUR with their hair and beard uncut; and that they should wear turbans instead of caps or scarves.

By noon, well over twenty thousand Sikhs (eighty thousand by one estimate) had assembled in the fairground at ANANDPUR to participate in the festivities of the BAISAKHI DAY. Everybody was excited and looked forward to meeting the GURU as if this unusual 'message' was especially sent for him. Also, there was a large and richly festooned tent pitched on a hillock overlooking the extensive fairgrounds.

It was afternoon. Word went round that the Guru was in the marquee and he would be coming out soon to meet his Sikhs. All eyes were turned towards the tent and everyone was waiting patiently for GURU'S DARSHAN (appearance) and to receive his blessings. But it took a little longer than expected.

At last their patience was rewarded. Guru Gobind came out of the tent clad in a strangely coloured uniform. It was saffron coloured from top to toe with a blue waistband. There was a long sword hanging from his left side. He walked briskly and came to a specially erected platform near the tent. The skies were clear and bright; and the Guru seemed to be standing so near, although he was actually at some distance from the people in the back. He had a strange smile on his face. Suddenly he stopped staring at the crowd, he pulled his sword out and raised it high with his right hand. There were 'a million voices' and then a sudden hush.

Now, like a thunder, the Guru spoke: "My dear Sikhs, I am glad to see so many of you here today. Today I have planned to offer you something special. But for this I need your help. Indeed, I need your head. I need the head of a Sikh who claims his faith in me."

There was a deadly silence all around. Everybody was too stunned to walk away or even whisper. Then the Guru flashed his sword again, raised his voice and repeated, "My Sikhs, I want a head, and nothing less than a head. If anyone among you claims to be a true Sikh, then come forward and prove it." He looked so fierce and bloodthirsty.

Before he had finished his last sentence, a tall lean Sikh was already moving forward towards the Guru on the platform. His name was DAYA RAM, a Khatri(shop owner)from LAHORE. Reaching the Guru, he folded his hands, bent his head forward and said, "O, Lord, the True Guru, I claim to be your humble Sikh. My head is ready for you. Please take it".

Hurriedly, the Guru held him by the arm and led him into the tent. Soon after the crowd outside heard the sound of a sword striking a body. They heard a voice, WAHEGURU and then a loud thud. Then they saw the GURU coming out of the tent, looking even more fierce. Fresh blood dripped down his sword. The crowd was totally horrified. Nobody needed to be told what had happened inside the tent.

Once again the Guru stood on the platform. Once again he raised his sword and addressed the crowd, "Well, my Sikhs! I want a second Sikh who would willingly offer his head to me." This new demand made the people even more frightened. But they dare not ask or challenge the Guru for his seemingly wrongful act. However, as he was repeating his strange call, another Sikh began to move forward. His name was DHARAM DAS, and he was a Jat (farmer) from Delhi.

Dharam Das stood before the Guru and said in a humble voice, "O, my true king, I offer my head to you, please take it, it is yours." Now the Guru seemed pleased as he quickly took him inside the tent. This time again, the crowd heard a voice saying WAHEGURU and then a loud thud. Everyone gasped. They were sure that Dharam Das, too, had been put to death.

Guru Gobind Singh creates Khalsa

"I need the head of a Sikh who claims his faith in me."

Then he himself was baptised by 'the five' and was called GOBIND SINGH.

Again the Guru emerged from the tent with a sword drenched in blood. He looked as fierce as before. With a terrifying look in his eyes he again shouted to the crowd, "Come, come my Sikhs, who comes next. I still want some more. Now I want a third head. I want a Sikh who has faith in me."

The people were terrified. They thought perhaps the Guru had gone mad. He was asking too much. Now they were no longer spellbound by the events which had taken place just before. They could think. They began to move; they whispered with each other. They began to slip away from the crowd. Some just fled for their lives.

In the meantime another Sikh named MOKHAN CHAND had reached the Guru on the platform. He was a Dhobi (washerman) from DWARKA. With folded hands he requested the Guru to accept his head. The Guru did not wait or waste a minute, and did the same as he had done with the other two.

For the fourth time, the Guru stood before the crowd and repeated his demand for yet another head. Now the crowd was even more restless. Some people were slinking away but most stood their ground. They were all really frightened, and it did not take long before they saw yet another Sikh on the platform offering his head to the Guru. His name was SAHIB CHAND and he was a barber from BIDAR. The Guru dealt with him in the same way as with the other three before him.

The crowd was getting thinner every moment. By the time the Guru came back and asked for a fifth head, only the very faithful had stayed behind. But there seemed to be no shortage of volunteers. Soon, another Sikh, a water-carrier from JAGAN-NATH named HIMMAT RAI moved forward. He was at once led to the tent, but this time the Guru did not return quickly. The people outside began to wonder. Their horror began to change into hope. At least the Guru had stopped asking for more heads. They waited nervously and prayed 'WAHEGURU'. 'WAHEGURU'. (Lit. means wonderful Lord i.e. God)

Then the Guru appeared. He was followed by five other men. They too were dressed in saffron colour, with blue scarves tied round their waists, and turbans. They looked very much like the Guru himself. All stood on the platform facing the crowd. Their faces beamed with joy and satisfaction.

As soon as the people near them recognised that they were the same Sikhs who they thought had been killed by the Guru, they immediately started cheering and saluting them with loud shouts of 'SAT SIRI AKAL!' Soon everybody joined in, and the whole atmosphere was vibrant with the deafening sounds of SAT SIRI AKAL. Many people who had left the fairground in fear and disappointment heard these cheers and rushed back to see what was happening. They could not believe their eyes. Everything had happened so fast. They could not understand. 'Had the dead been brought back to life?'

When the cheering had stopped, the Guru spoke to the crowd, "My dear Sikhs; we all remember that when Guru Nanak gave a test to his Sikhs only one passed it. His name was LEHNA, who then became Guru Angad. Now two hundred years after the first test, I have given you another final test. However, this test is not for Guruship but for the 'nationhood'. I call it the KHALSA, the brotherhood of the pure at heart. You have witnessed the birth of the Khalsa. These Sikhs standing beside me are my PANJ PIARAY (five beloved ones). Each of them is a saint and a soldier in one. These five Sikhs are dedicated and daring enough to lead; and strong enough to support the edifice of the Khalsa."

Later the Guru introduced his Sikhs to a new kind of initiation ceremony called the AMRIT (see page 44).

First he baptised the 'PANJ PIARAY' and gave them a new name — 'SINGH'. Then he himself was baptised by 'the five' and called himself GOBIND SINGH. After this all Sikhs present at the fairground were asked to receive AMRIT. It was estimated that well over 20,000 Sikhs were baptised the same day.

FROM PERSECUTION TO POWER

With the birth of the Khalsa came the wrath of the Emperor of Delhi and the local princes, who saw something sinister in the mass baptism of the Sikhs on the Baisakhi Day. The relative peace which the Sikhs had enjoyed by keeping a low profile during the last two decades was suddenly over. Emperor Aurangzeb instructed the Governor of Panjab to dispossess Guru Gobind Singh of his people and property at ANANDPUR. Thus Anandpur was soon besieged by the Mughal Armies and the Guru was forced to leave the place along with his wife, children and other Sikhs.

Thereupon many battles were fought between the Khalsa and the royal armies chasing the Guru. During the course of the war the Guru lost all his four sons, his mother and countless other Sikhs. But this did not deter other Sikhs joining his ranks, the most important of them was one named BANDA SINGH, popularly known as BANDA BAHADUR, whom he appointed as the commander of his armies. Guru Gobind Singh died of stab wounds in 1708, a year after the death of Emperor Aurangzeb.

The next sixty years of Sikh history were a period of extreme hardship, suffering and religious persecution. At one time between 1740-50, people were offered rewards by the Governor of the Panjab for hunting down Sikhs — '5 rupees for information, 10 rupees after arrest, 15 rupees for a severed head and 50 rupees for bringing a Sikh alive to the police station.' (Foster, a contemporary Briton, in his book 'Journey from Bengal').

These events made the Sikhs even more daring and revengeful. All able-bodied male Sikhs joined the Khalsa armies and camped in the forests of the Panjab. Soon they became masters of guerrilla warfare. The persecutions and executions of most of the Sikh women and children left behind simply increased their hatred for the Mughal Government and made them more determined to take revenge.

According to Malcolm, another chronicle writer, "The Sikh nation, throughout their early history, have always appeared like a suppressed flame to rise into higher splendour from every attempt to crush them." A contemporary Muslim historian wrote in his book 'Ibrat Namah Alla - Ud - Din' that the Sikhs used to sing:

"Mannu cuts us with a sickle, and we are his crop of 'SOAY',
The more he cuts us the more we grow, in every house or hut."

By the year 1765, the Mughal Empire had lost much of its power and glory. The Abdali invasions from the west, the Marathas from the south and the British influence from the east, all helped to weaken the strength of the Delhi Government. This was an opportune time for the Sikhs to seize power in the Panjab.

This they did before the end of 1767 when they chased away AHMED SHAH ABDALI across the Indus River to Afghanistan and also killed Sarfraz Khan, the Governor of the Panjab. They then divided themselves into 12 MISALS (confederacies) each controlled by a powerful chief. The system of administration and justice was then completely re-organised. Complete religious freedom was granted and capital punishment abolished.

An eminent Hindu historian, Gokal Chand Narang thus writes in his book called 'Transformation of Sikhism':

"The nation started with a rosary and ended by snatching the sceptre from the oppressing hand of its tyrannical masters. The political organisation of the Sikhs was now complete and the sovereignty of the land of five waters had now permanently passed to the children of the Khalsa to keep in custody for a great power."

THE RISE AND EXTENT OF SIKH POWER

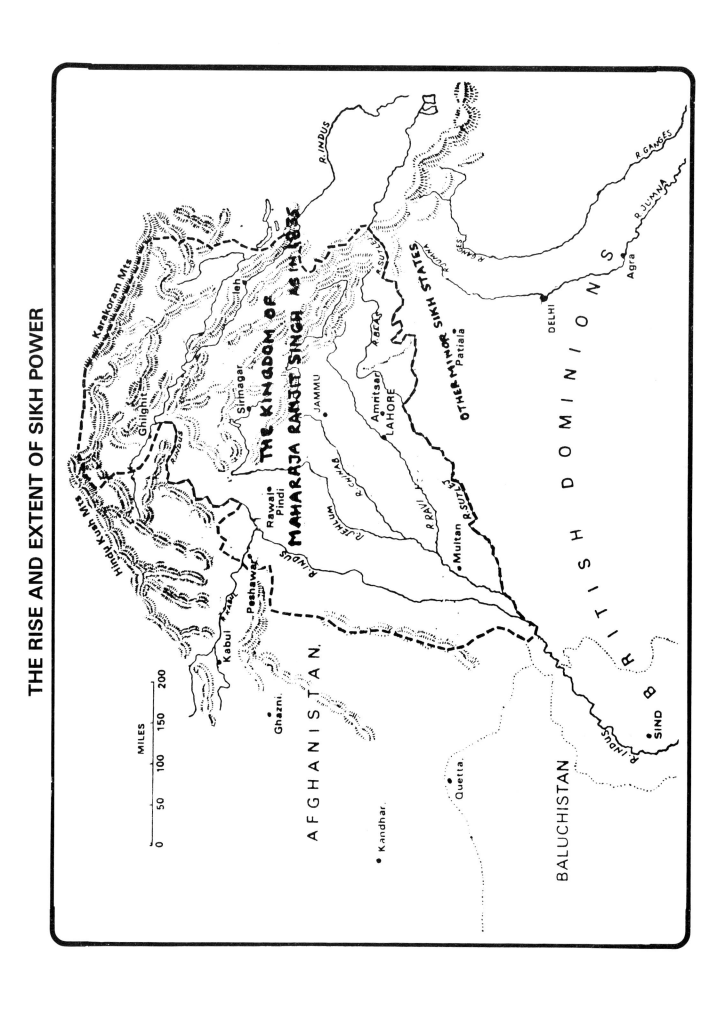

MAHARAJA RANJIT SINGH

(1780—1839)

MAHARAJA RANJIT SINGH

Maharaja Ranjit Singh is also popularly known as the 'Lion of the Panjab' for his extraordinary courage, stamina and generous character. A born ruler and with a natural genius of command, he soon realised that rivalry and disputes among the Sikh chiefs ruling different confederacies were inevitable. Thus he carried out the task of abolishing the confederacies and himself sat on the throne of Lahore. From 1797 until his death in 1839, Ranjit Singh extended and consolidated his empire, annexing Kashmir and the N.W. Frontier including the Khyber.

How others saw him

Victor Jacquemont ('Letters from India', 1834)
"The Panjab and its inhabitants please me much. Perhaps you will say that it is because I see them through a shower of gold; but the unsophisticated Sikhs of this country have a simplicity and open honesty of manner which a European relishes the more after two years' residence or travelling in India."

"His (Ranjit Singh's) conversation is like a nightmare. He is almost the first inquisitive Indian I have seen . . . . He asked a hundred thousand questions to me about India, the British, Europe, Bonaparte, this world in general and the next, hell, paradise, the soul, God, the devil and a myriad of others of the same kind."

Captain W. Murray ('History of the Panjab', 1846)
"Ranjit Singh has been likened to Mehemet Ali and to Napoleon. Mr. Jacquemont terms him "a Bonaparte in miniature." There are some points in which he resembles both; but estimating his character with reference to his circumstances and position, he is perhaps a more remarkable man than either."

"It is difficult to suppress admiration in contemplating the career of such a man, who, with so many disadvantages, succeeded, with so few crimes, in elevating himself from a simple Sardar to be the Sovereign of a large kingdom, including Hindus and Mohammadans, as well as Sikhs, the only state in India not substantially under British dominion."

Alex Gardner ('Soldier and Traveller — Memoirs of Alex Gardner' 1898)
"The Maharaja was indeed one of those master-minds which only require opportunity to change the face of the globe. Ranjit Singh made a great and powerful nation from the disunited confederacies of the Sikhs and would have carried his conquests to Delhi or even farther, had it not been for the simultaneous rise and consolidation of the British Empire in India."

Lt.-Col Steinbach ('The Panjab', 1846)
"The treasure (of Maharaja Ranjit Singh) may be estimated to have amounted at his decease to about eight 'crore' of rupees in cash, or the same number of millions of pounds sterling, with jewels, shawls, horses, elephants etc, and several million more . . . . . . it is doubtful if any Court in Europe possesses such valuable jewels as the Court of Lahore."

Gokal Chand Narang ('Transformation of Sikhism').
". . . . . . and the highest posts in his Government were as open to the Mussalmans as to the Sikhs and Hindus. His most trusted minister was Fakir Ajiz-Ud-Din (a Muslim) . . . . . In fact . . . . . all his ministers were either Rajputs, Brahmans or Mussalmans . . . . . . The Maharaja had several Europeans and some Americans also in his service. They were engaged in training his troops on European lines and did their work so well that the Sikh troops became the most efficient fighting force in India and were compared to Cromwell's Ironsides".

THE FALL OF THE SIKH RAJ

When Maharaja Ranjit Singh died in 1839, the agents of the British East India Company had already started making clever plans to annex the last remaining independent territory in India. Very soon special cantonments were set up along the border with Panjab, and the seeds of dissent and dissatisfaction were sown among the contenders for the throne of Lahore as well as among ministers and generals.

By 1843, within a period of four years all important male members of the Royal Family were killed one after the other. The only surviving member was a young prince named Duleep Singh. He was six now, and was proclaimed as the Maharaja with his mother Maharani Jind Kaur acting as regent.

Similarly, there was tough infighting and rivalry for the Prime Ministership. Two Hindu Sardars, namely Dian Singh and Gulab Singh, had their own plans ready which also suited their English 'friends' very much as was evident from Lord Harding's letters[1] to his wife Emily Harding. Besides, two other candidates were equally corrupt and selfish. The result was the Anglo-Sikh wars of 1845-46 and 1848-49, the details of which, although extremely interesting, are not relevant in the present context.

By the end of 1850, the young Prince Duleep Singh was removed and his kingdom formally annexed to the British Empire. At first he was exiled from Panjab to Fatehgarh in U.P. (India) where he was converted to Christianity on 8th March, 1853. Then he was taken to England in 1854, where he spent practically the rest of his life. In the eighties of the last century, frustrated and disgusted by his treatment in England, he left for India but was held at Aden and brought back. However, during his short stay at Aden he renounced Christianity and reconverted to Sikhism by receiving AMRIT. Vainly, he tried to seek assistance from Russia and eventually died of a broken heart in Paris on October 22, 1893.[2]

---

[1] Extracts from Lord Harding's letters to his wife Emily Harding.

10th February, 1846 : "I have a communication from Raja Gulab Singh which may lead to overtures for an arrangement; he is to be made a minister and says he is ready to do whatever we like to order."

19th February, 1846 : "well, I have the ablest scoundrel in all Asia close to my camp — the Wazir Raja Gulab Singh — a good-looking, clever-eyed man of 50 and yesterday he brought the little Maharaja to my Durbar tent to make his submission and pay tribute."

1st March, 1846 : "I cannot say whether my policy in dealing with the Sikh nation will be approved or not . . . I have annexed a very rich district bounded by the river Beas to the Indian Empire chiefly to improve our frontiers . . . . . . I have made all the hill tribes touching our hill frontier independent of the Sikhs . . . . . I have placed all these countries under a Rajput dynasty chief called Raja Gulab Singh who is by religion a Hindu."

[2]
Elveden Hall, Thetford, Suffolk
The Place or 'Palace' where Maharaja Duleep Singh lived most of his life and was later wrongfully* 'buried' after his death. (Occasionally Sikhs remember him by visiting the place.)

*Sikhs do not bury but cremate their dead.

PRINCE DULEEP SINGH (The Maharaja in exile)

SIKH FESTIVALS AND HOLY DAYS

Sikhs do not believe that any particular day of the week is a HOLY DAY. However, SANGRAAND (the first day of the Indian lunar calendar month) is an important day, when most Sikhs like to visit the Gurdwara for special prayers, usually in the early morning.

In India most Gurdwaras are open to the public for prayer and worship all day and every day; special congregational services are held both in the early morning and evening.

In Britain, Sunday being a holiday, most Sikhs find it convenient to visit a Gurdwara on that day. However, at some places Saturday evening is regarded as convenient.

A Sikh festival or a holy-day is called a GURPURB. Gurpurb means the GURU'S Remembrance Day. This usually refers to the birth or the death of Gurus. The following Gurpurbs are regarded as rather important:

i)   Guru Nanak's Birthday (usually in November)
ii)   Guru Gobind Singh's Birthday (end December or early January)
iii) The Birthday of the Khalsa (mid April)
iv)   Guru Arjan's Martyrdom (usually in June)
v)   Guru Teg Bahadur's Martyrdom (usually in October)
vi)   Guru Granth Parkash (end August or early September)

The Birth of Guru Nanak

This 'Gurpurb' comes, usually, in the month of November and is celebrated with great excitement. An important feature of the celebration is a colourful procession of hundreds and thousands of Sikh men, women and children which is led by the PANJ PIARAY (five beloved ones) and the HOLY GRANTH on a float. As the procession winds its way through the streets a continuous chant of the sacred music or hymn singing is heard, which is occasionally broken by loud shouts of salutations of SAT SIRI AKAL (Hail Victory to the True Lord).

In most Gurdwaras celebrations start a couple of days earlier with the commencement of AKHAND-PATH (non-stop reading of the Holy Granth for 48 hours). On the final day, the atmosphere in and around the Gurdwara is like a fair, as families and groups of Sikhs are seen entering and leaving the premises throughout the day.

In the evening, some Sikhs illuminate their homes and shops with candles, 'deevas' or other electric lights. Occasionally, a display of fireworks is also arranged, especially at the Gurdwaras. However, the most spectacular sight is the DARBAR SAHIB (Golden Temple), AMRITSAR, which as on DIWALI NIGHT looks like a floating palace of multicoloured lights.

BAISAKHI (or VAISAKHI)

This festive day or the Gurpurb celebrating the birth of the 'Khalsa' usually falls on 13th April. Baisakhi was originally celebrated to mark the beginning of the New Year (according to the ancient Indian Lunar Calendar).

To the Sikhs, the importance of this day is both historical and religious. It was on this day on 13th April, 1699, that Guru Gobind Singh gave the Sikhs a new name (SINGH) and a new identity of being a nation, by making them distinctively different in physical appearance and personal behaviour. Henceforth, along with 'inner discipline' the Sikhs were asked to keep an 'outer discipline' too by wearing the 5Ks. The full story of the Birth of the Khalsa is described elsewhere in this book.

BAISAKHI is also an important harvest festival in the Panjab. All over the Panjab farmers are happy because they have gathered in the wheat, the most important crop of the season . Now they can perform BHANGRA (folk dance) and sing. The folklore goes like this —

> "O, Jatta aayee visakhi,
> Kanka di muk gayee rakhi."

Meaning — Hey! farmer! the Baisakhi has come and you no longer need to worry about and watch your wheat fields.

DIWALI

Although essentially a Hindu festival, the Sikhs have found themselves enough good reasons to celebrate this day as another important festival. The most popular one is that on this day Guru Hargobind, the sixth Guru, arrived in Amritsar after his release from FORT GWALIOR where he was imprisoned by the Moghal Emperor, Johangir. Diwali is commonly known as the festival of lights or lamps. Thus many Sikh homes and business properties are decorated and lit with **DEEVAS** (oil lamps made of clay), candles and multicoloured electric bulbs. Children look forward to enjoying fireworks and family feasts. The Darbar Sahib at Amritsar presents another spectacular sight at night, with hundreds and thousands of big and small oil lamps, candles and electric lights. Usually, Diwali falls in the month of October.

LOHRRI, MAGHI and **HOLI** are other popular festivals of Panjab. They have no real religious significance to the Sikhs, except locally, and generally their celebrations coincide with a particular season.

However, there are quite a few other local fairs which are historically important to the Sikhs and attract crowds in hundreds of thousands and last two to three days. The most important of these are:

i)   **HOLA MAHALLA** at **ANANDPUR SAHIB**

ii)   **THE MARTYRDOM** of two younger **SAHIBZADAS** (sons) of Guru Gobind Singh at **FATEH GARH SAHIB** — near Sirhind.

iii)   The Battle of **MUKATSAR**

iv)   The Battle of **CHAMKAUR SAHIB** and the Martyrdom of two elder **SAHIBZADAS**

HOLA MAHALLA Procession at ANANDPUR SAHIB

30

TWO SPECIMENS OF SIKH GREETING CARDS
(Inside page only)

ੴ

ਮੈ ਹੈ ਪਰਮ ਪਰਖ ਕੇ ਦਾਸਾ॥
ਦੇਖਨ ਆਏ ਜਗਤ ਤਮਾਸਾ॥

ਗੁਰੂ ਗੋਬਿੰਦ ਸਿੰਘ ਜੀ

ਸ੍ਰੀ ਗੁਰੂ ਗੋਬਿੰਦ ਸਿੰਘ ਜੀ
ਮਹਾਰਾਜ ਦੇ ਅਵਤਾਰ
ਗੁਰਪੁਰਬ
ਅਤੇ ਨਵੇਂ ਸਾਲ ਦੀ

ਵਧਾਈ

EK-ON-KAR

I am the servant of the
Supreme Being;
Ordained to witness the
World Pageant.

(GURU GOBIND SINGH JI)

Heartiest Greetings
on the
Birth Anniversary of
Guru Gobind Singh Ji
&
A Happy New Year

31

ਖਾਲਸਾ ਮੇਰੋ ਰੂਪ ਹੈ ਖਾਸ ।
Khalsa is my own special form

ਖਾਲਸੇ ਮਾਹਿ ਹੈ ਕਰੋਂ ਨਿਵਾਸ ॥
I always manifest in the Khalsa

ਜਾਗਤ ਜੋਤ ਜਪੈ ਨਿਸ ਬਾਸੁਰ,
And he who repeats the name of the omnipresent day and night

ਏਕ ਬਿਨਾ ਮਨ ਨੇਕ ਨ ਆਨੈ ।
Sets not his thoughts on any other but one almighty.

ਪੂਰਨ ਪ੍ਰੇਮ ਪ੍ਰਤੀਤ ਸਜੇ, ਧ੍ਰੁਤ
Who is ever imbued with his presence everywhere.

ਗੋਰ ਮੜੀ ਮਟ ਭੂਲ ਨਾ ਮਾਨੈ ।
And observes (believes) no fast and bows not to the graves.

ਤੀਰਥ, ਦਾਨ, ਦਯਾ, ਤਪ, ਸੰਜਮ,
Who attaches little value to pilgrimages and austerities.

ਏਕ ਬਿਨਾ ਨਹਿ ਏ ਪਛਾਨੈ ।
And recognises the authority only of one God.

ਪੂਰਨ ਜੋਤਿ ਜਗੈ ਘਟ ਮੈ
In his blessed heart will dwell the perfect Lord.

ਤਬ ਖਾਲਸਾ ਤਾਹਿ ਨਖਾਲਸ ਜਾਨੈ ।
And only he deserves to be called "Khalsa".

ਜਬ ਲਗ ਖਾਲਸਾ ਰਹੇ ਨਿਆਰਾ
As long as Khalsa remains distinctive

ਤਬ ਲਗ ਤੇਜ ਦੀਉ ਮੈਂ ਸਾਰਾ।
I shall bestow glory on him.

Vaisakhi Greetings

and
Best wishes on the auspicious occasion
of
The Birth of Khalsa

(Specimens of Sikh Greeting Cards — inside page, issued at the time of
(a) the Birth of Guru Gobind Singh and the coming of New Year,
(b) the Birth of Khalsa and the coming of Spring.

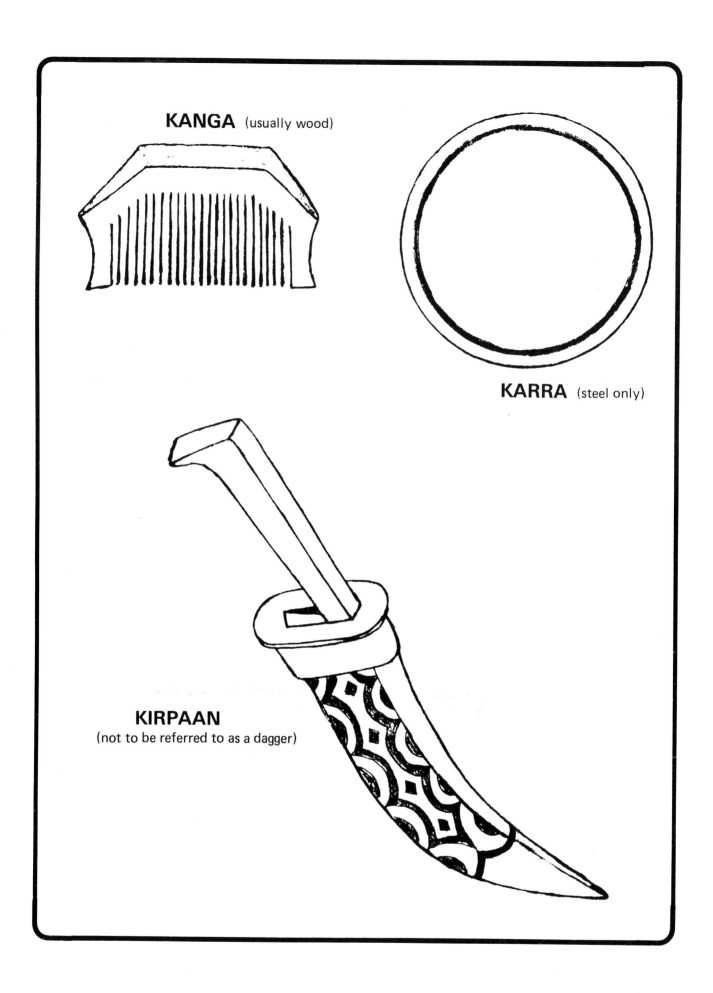

KANGA (usually wood)

KARRA (steel only)

KIRPAAN
(not to be referred to as a dagger)

THE SIKH TURBAN AND THE FIVE Ks.

The most important and noticeable thing about Sikhs is their distinctiveness in appearance, especially because of a turban and well kept long hair and beard.

Guru Nanak himself started this tradition of keeping hair intact and covering the head with a turban. The rest of the Nine Gurus encouraged their Sikhs to do the same. The following quotation from the ADI GRANTH (Sikh Holy Book) clearly shows that long before Guru Gobind Singh made it obligatory, the keeping of long hair and the wearing of a turban was actively preached by all the Gurus.

> *"Let living in His presence,*
> *With mind rid of impurities,*
> *Be your discipline.*
> *Keep the God-given form intact,*
> *With a turban donned on your head."*   (Adi Granth, P.1084-Line 12)

However, it was Guru Gobind Singh who introduced a unique form of baptism, 'AMRIT', for the Sikhs and asked that they wear certain outfits as a matter of Sikh discipline or uniform. This uniform consists of five 'articles of faith' known as The Five Ks. Naturally, for Sikhs these are essentially religious symbols which have deep spiritual significance; and some practical as well. The five Ks are called 'KAKKAAR', because each of them begins with the letter 'K'. They are:

1. KESH
Kesh means hair. Sikhs should treat their hair as a gift from God Himself. It is His trust. To keep this God-given form intact is the first and foremost duty of a Sikh. The hair is a symbol of faith, and keeping long hair confirms a Sikh's belief in the acceptance of God's Will, and teaches them HUMILITY and ACCEPTANCE.

2. KANGHA
Kangha means comb. Sikhs use a small wooden comb (as shown in the picture) because it can be worn easily in the hair all the time. Apart from its practical utility, a comb is clearly a symbol of cleanliness. Just as a comb helps to remove the tangles and cleans the hair, similarly Sikhs are reminded to get rid of any impurities of thought by repeating 'NAAM' (God's name) in their mind.

3. KARRA
Karra literally means a link or bond. It is a special (ridged) steel bracelet which is worn on the right wrist like a wedding ring which signifies a bond between the two people. The Karra is the Guru's own symbolic ring to all his Sikhs signifying their unbreakable link or bond with the Guru as well as among themselves, belonging to the brotherhood of Khalsa. Also the circle is a symbol of restraint, and in practice a constant reminder to the Sikh of ideal behaviour in the event of weakness.

4. KACHHA
Kachha is a pair of shorts. This is a special, slightly longer type of underwear and is symbolic of continence and a high moral character. Like breeches, Kachha can be worn on their own without causing embarrassment. Thus they are quite useful in hot weather, and for swimming and sports activities.

5. KIRPAAN
Kirpaan is a sword. However, Sikhs only ever call it the Kirpaan. Kirpaan comes from the word KIRPA and AAN. Kirpa means an act of kindness, a favour; and 'aan' means honour, respect, self-respect. It is an instrument which adds to self-respect and self-defence. Thus for Sikhs, Kirpaan is the symbol of power and freedom of spirit. All baptised Sikhs should wear a short form of Kirpaan (approx. 6" x 9" long) on their body. To call it a dagger or a knife is rather insulting this article of faith, which functions quite differently from the other two.

> *"He alone is my true disciple, friend, kinsman and brother,*
> *Who accepts the Guru's discipline;*
> *He who is guided by his own ego O brother,*
> *Is separated from the Lord and gets no comfort."*   (The Adi Granth P.601—line 18)

> *"He alone is my real Sikh, who lives up to the Sikh Form*   (Guru Gobind Singh)
> *He is my master and I am his follower."*

THE SIKH TURBAN

The turban is commonly associated with India because of the popular belief that most of the Indians wear turbans — which is not true. Hardly 10% of the total male population of India may wear turbans regularly.

Again, in India, Sikhs constitute only 1.8% of the total population and as such any turbanned Indian you see behind the plough or in the street is not necessarily a SIKH.

Although essentially religious, the SIKH TURBAN, in practical terms, is not without merits. The turban is more hygienic than a hat or cap which is difficult to wash clean. It is made up of fine muslin (cotton) which is kept clean with the usual weekly washing.

The turban is always a made-to-measure thing. That is — it fits the contour or shape of the head, and so is more comfortable than the ready-made or factory made hats which are usually the same shape for all differently featured heads.

Contrary to what many people think, the turban is light (a few ounces only) and soft on the head, but its cushion-like appearance may give the wrong impression of being bulky or heavy.

Acting like a vacuum flask, it is ideal headgear for both winter and summer. Even in icy winds it keeps the head and ears cosy and comfortable, while under the hot, perspiring sun it also has more utility than many people would realise.

For all jobs requiring a certain uniform, such as a conductor or driver, a postman or policeman, the turban is perhaps the best uniform for the head where it makes a snug fit, and cannot easily be knocked off or blown away.

The turban can act as a safety cushion. In ordinary daily life — driving a car or riding a bike, walking on the road or having a joyride at a funfair — the turban certainly provides reasonable safety to the head from any sudden accident. It should be remembered that it is precisely in ordinary daily life that most accidents occur — i.e. when we are least prepared to protect our head.

Apart from providing some safety at all times, the turban is an automatic and suitable hair cover while working in such areas as a food factory or an operating theatre, a kitchen or canteen.

For variety and taste, there is a choice of colours. Match it with your suit, shirt, or necktie — there is no restriction to any colour. However, blue and white are particular favourites with certain Sikhs; e.g. white with Sikhs from East Africa and dark blue with 'Akalis' — members of a Sikh political party called AKALI DAL.

Other things being equal, the 'Sikh Turban' is inexpensive to buy and easy to make. In England it now costs about £5.00 and is in plentiful supply at Asian shops. Learning and mastering the tying of turban is a gentle and natural process from children to adults. Usually, a boy of 8 or 10 years of age acquires the initial skill in making his own turban; to him it is perhaps as easy or as difficult as lacing up his boots or tying up his necktie unaided by his parents.

Usually an adult Sikh Turban is five metres long and one metre wide. This length is smoothly turned around the head six times (rounds) by clockwise movements of the hands. Both ends of the 'length' or the turban must be tucked in properly — i.e. the beginning or finishing ends of the turban should not be flowing loosely as can be seen with many non-Sikh Indian turbans.

Most Sikhs prefer to wear another small under-turban as well, just as we use underwear, and it is usually white. This under-turban may be kept on at bed-time as well, when the turban proper is taken off. Similarly, during swimming and sports, the turban is replaced by a small scarf called 'PATKA' or handkerchief which is knotted at the top to keep the hair intact. In fact PATKA is becoming more popular with young Sikhs at school.

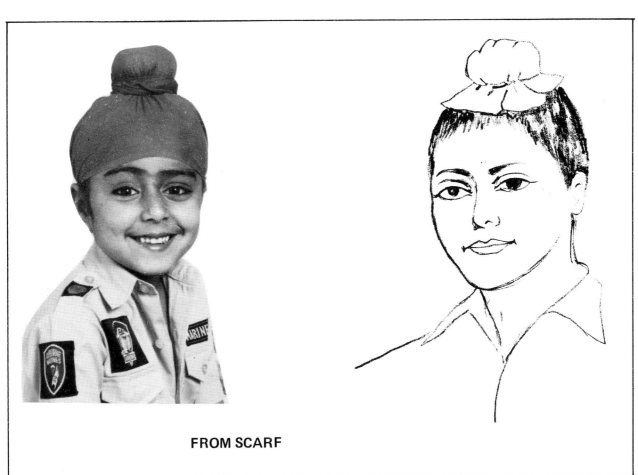

FROM SCARF

TO TURBAN

THE SIKH RELIGIOUS SYMBOLS AND THE LAW

JEK

HOME OFFICE
Queen Anne's Gate London SW1H 9AT

Direct line 01-213
Switchboard 01-213 3000

Our reference

QPE/76 141/5/64
Date 4 June 1979

Dear Mr Mayer

Thank you for your letter of 22 May to the Home Secretary forwarding a copy of a Resolution passed at your General Council Meeting on 25 April concerning the Sikh holy symbols - the 5 K's.

I can assure you that the police are well aware of the significance of the Sikh religious symbols. It is certainly no offence merely to carry or wear an article such as a Sikh Kara or Kirpan, though it could be an offence under the Prevention of Crime Act 1953 to use, or intend to use, such an article as an offensive weapon. (Section 1 of the Act makes it an offence for any person to have with him in a public place any offensive weapon without lawful authority or reasonable excuse. An "offensive weapon" is defined as "any article made or adapted for use for causing injury to the person or intended by the person having it with him for such use by him").

Yours sincerely

Mrs D S walters

Photocopy by courtesy of the Council for Racial Equality (London Borough of Barking & Dagenham)

KIRPAN IS NOT A WEAPON: Jakhar

NEW DELHI, Nov 19 (U.N.I.) — "Kirpan is not a weapon. It is a religious symbol", said speaker Bal Ram Jakhar in the Lok Sabha* today.

He was replying to a point of order raised by Mr. Ram Nagina Mishra when Akali Dal member Mr. Tarlochan Singh Tur took the oath in the House with a kirpan dangling from his waist.

Mr. Mishra asked whether any member could come to the House carrying a weapon.

Mr. Jakhar assured Mr. Mishra that no one was permitted to come to the House with a weapon.

(*House of Commons, Parliament of India) November 19, 1985.

Motor-Cycle Crash Helmets
(Religious Exemption) Act, 1976

1976 CHAPTER 62

An Act to exempt turban-wearing followers of the Sikh religion from the requirement to wear a crash-helmet when riding a motor-cycle. (15th November 1976)

BE IT ENACTED by the Queen's most Excellent Majesty, by and with the advice and consent of the Lords Spiritual and Temporal, and Commons, in this present Parliament assembled, and by the authority of the same, as follows:—

1. In section 32 of the Road Traffic Act 1972 there shall be inserted after subsection (2) the following new subsection:

"(2A) A requirement imposed by regulations under this section (whenever made) shall not apply to any follower of the Sikh religion while he is wearing a turban."

2. This Act may be cited as the Motor-Cycle Crash-Helmets (Religious Exemption) Act 1976.

Extracts from the Delhi Sikh Gurdwara Act,* 1971 passed by the Parliament of Republic of India

"SIKH"

"Sikh" means a person who professes the Sikh religion, believes and follows the teachings of Sri Guru Granth Sahib and the ten Gurus only and keeps unshorn hair. For the purposes of this Act, if any question arises as to whether any living person is or is not a Sikh he shall be deemed respectively to be or not to be a Sikh according as he makes or refuses to make the manner prescribed by rules the following declaration:-

"I solemnly affirm that I am a Keshadhari Sikh, that I believe in and follow the teaching of Sri Guru Granth Sahib and the ten Gurus only, and that I have no other religion".

"AMRITDHARI SIKH"

"Amritdhari Sikh" means and includes every Sikh who has taken Khande Ka Amrit or Khanda Pahul, prepared and administered according to the tenets of Sikh religion and rites at the hands of five Pyaras or "beloved ones".

"PATIT"

"Patit" means a Sikh who trims or shaves his beard or hair (Keshas) or who after taking Amrit commits any one or more of the four Kurahitis.* (*These are given on page 41 under INJUNCTIONS)

---

*as derived from the Sikh Gurdwara Act 1925

THE SIKH INSIGNIA

THE KHANDA

I The **KHANDA** is the insignia of the SIKHS. It constitutes three symbols in one. However, the name is derived from the central symbol, Khanda, which is a special type of double-edged sword resembling figure 1. This symbolises the ONLY ONE, the SUPREME TRUTH, the CREATOR, and thus confirms the SIKHS' belief in ONE GOD.

II Next, the CHAKKAR, or the circle, represents the infiniteness of the TIMELESS ABSOLUTE. The circle is also symbolic of restraint and a reminder to a Sikh to stay within the rule of God.

III Of the two KIRPAANS, or swords, on the sides, one is symbolic of PEERI (spiritual authority) and the other of MEERI (political or temporal power).

NISHAN SAHIB (THE SIKH FLAG)

The **SIKH FLAG** is a saffron-coloured triangular-shaped cloth, usually reinforced in the middle and with the Sikh insignia in blue. It is usually mounted on a long steel pole (which is also covered with the same coloured cloth) headed with a khanda. The Sikh flag is often seen near the entrance to the GURDWARA, standing firmly on the THARRA (platform) overlooking the whole building. Sikhs show great respect to their flag as it is, indeed, the symbol of the freedom of the KHALSA— political and religious.

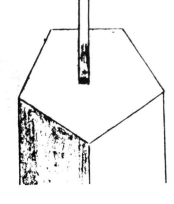

ਦੇਹ ਸ਼ਿਵਾ ਬਰ ਮੋਹਿ ਇਹੈ
DEH SHIVA BAR MOHE IHAI

Grant me this boon
O, God, from Thy Greatness

ਸ਼ੁਭ ਕਰਮਨ ਤੇ ਕਬਹੂੰ ਨ ਟਰੋਂ ॥
SHUBH KARMAN TEY KABHU NA TAROO

May I never refrain
From righteous acts;

ਨਾ ਡਰੋ ਅਰਿ ਸਿਉ ਜਬ ਜਾਏ ਲਰੋ
NA DAROO AR SIYOO JAB JAH LAROO

May I fight without fear
All foes in life's battle,

ਨਿਸਚੈ ਕਰ ਆਪਨੀ ਜੀਤ ਕਰੋ ॥
NISCHAI KR APNI JEET KAROO

With confident courage
Claiming the victory!

ਅਰੁ ਸਿਖਹੋਂ ਆਪਨੇ ਹੀ ਮਨ ਕੈ
AR SIKH HAO APNE HI MUN KO

May Thy glory be
Grained in my mind,

ਇਹ ਲਾਲਚ ਹਉ ਗੁਣ ਤਉ ਉਚਰੋਂ
EH LALACH HOU GUNA TAU UCHROO

And my highest ambition be
Singing Thy praises;

ਜਬ ਆਵ ਕੀ ਅਉਧ ਨਿਧਾਨ ਬਨੈ
JAB AAV KI AUDH NIDHAAN BANAY

When this mortal life
Reaches its limits,

ਅਤਿ ਹੀ ਰਣ ਮੇ ਤਬ ਜੂਝ ਮਰੋਂ ॥
AUT HI RANN ME TAB JOOJH MAROO

May I die fighting
With limitless courage!

THE SIKH NATIONAL ANTHEM

The above composition is regarded as the **NATIONAL ANTHEM** of the **SIKHS**. The verses were composed by Guru Gobind Singh.

Guru Gobind Singh was a pillar of strength for the helpless and the down-trodden. From these humble people he created a new NATION and called it the KHALSA. He showed them the way to fight tyranny and injustice. While leading them in this crusade, he made supreme sacrifices which could hardly have any parallels in history. He lost his whole family — his father, mother and four sons, one by one. But nothing could deter him from the 'righteous acts'.

SUMMARY OF THE SIKH CODE OF CONDUCT

INSTRUCTIONS

1. THERE IS ONLY ONE GOD; WORSHIP AND PRAY TO HIM ALONE.

2. ALWAYS WORK HARD, AND SHARE WITH OTHERS.

3. PRACTISE TRUTH, AND LIVE A TRUTHFUL LIFE.

4. REMEMBER, WOMEN ARE AS GOOD AS MEN.

5. THE WHOLE HUMAN RACE IS ONE. DISTINCTIONS OF CASTE, COLOUR AND CLASS ARE WRONG. RESPECT OTHERS' CREED AS YOUR OWN.

6. IDOLS, MAGIC, OMENS, FASTS, FRONTAL MARKS AND SACRED THREADS ARE UNNECESSARY.

7. DRESS YOURSELF IN A SIMPLE AND MODEST WAY; GAUDY CLOTHES AND REVEALING DRESS BRING NO CREDIT.

8. SIKH WOMEN SHOULD NOT OBSERVE THE VEIL (PARDA); NEITHER SHOULD THEY OR MEN MAKE HOLES IN THEIR EARS AND NOSES.

9. LIVE A MARRIED LIFE; ASCETICISM AND RENUNCIATION ARE NEEDLESS EXERCISES.

10. PUT YOUR FAITH IN THE HOLY GRANTH; NO OTHER HOLY BOOK OR LIVING PERSON CAN CLAIM GURUSHIP (for Sikhs).

INJUNCTIONS   (GIVEN AT THE TIME OF INITIATION)

1. THOU SHALT NOT CUT HAIR.

2. THOU SHALT NOT USE TOBACCO*.

3. THOU SHALT NOT EAT RITUAL MEAT.

4. THOU SHALT NOT COMMIT ADULTERY.

*or any intoxicants

THE BASIC BELIEF

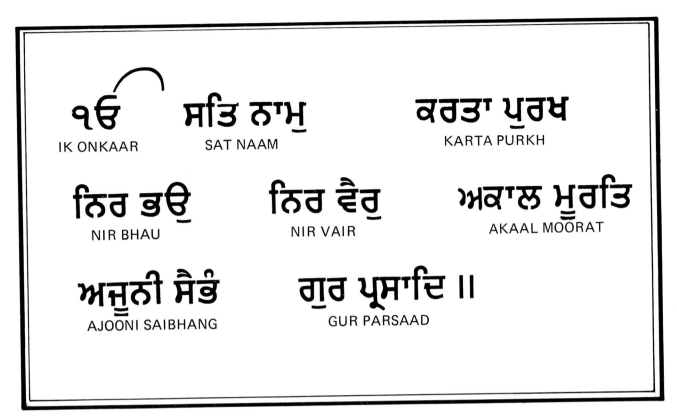

This is the **MOOL MANTAR**, the basic belief of the SIKHS. It begins in the beginning of HOLY GRANTH, and every Sikh is expected to recite it daily. Here is the English translation.

IK ONKAAR	There is one and only ONE GOD
SAT NAAM	TRUTH is HIS NAME
KARTA PURKH	He is the CREATOR
NIR BHAU	He is WITHOUT FEAR
NIR VAIR	He is WITHOUT HATE
AKAAL MOORAT	IMMORTAL/WITHOUT FORM
AJOONI	He is beyond birth and death
SAIBHANG	He is self illuminated (the Enlightener)
GUR PARSAAD	He is realised by the Kindness of the TRUE GURU.

THE ARDAS (the Sikh prayer)

The ARDAS is mainly a personal thing. It is being in direct communication with the Creator, Preserver and the Destroyer — WAHEGURU, The Lord.

Thus the ARDAS can vary in length and content. Sometimes in an informal and individual version only a few words are said, by way of saying grace before or after a meal, or starting on a journey. While on other more formal occasions like the conclusion of the Sikh Congregational Service, a standard version of about 35 or more sentences is recited. This is approximately 350-400 words, most of it in either verse or rhythmic prose and is thus easily committed to the memory of any person or priest leading the ARDAS.

Before the ARDAS begins, the whole congregation stands up facing the GURU GRANTH. All fold their hands before the chest and bow their heads in humility. First a SHABAD (hymn) from the Holy Granth is sung in chorus (see next page) and then the proper ARDAS is said by one person, while others follow silently (except saying one word WAHEGURU occasionally at the call of the leading person). This is like saying AMEN in a church prayer. At the end, again, before sitting down, another hymn composed by the 10th Guru Gobind Singh is sung in chorus, at the conclusion of which the leading priest calls out loudly — "JO BOLAY SO NIHAAL" and the whole congregation responds with one voice — "SAT SIRI AKAL"

(Blessed are those who say — IMMORTAL THE TRUE GOD).

Then all sit down and listen to a verse, chosen at random, from the Holy Granth. Finally, the KARAH PAR-SHAD (sacred sweet food) is served and the congregation disperses.

Extracts from the ARDAS

Line 1 "Having first remembered God the Almighty, think of Guru Nanak, ... "

Line 15-16 "Let the whole Khalsa bring to mind the Name of the wonderful Lord; and as s/he thinks of Him, may s/he feel completely blessed ...."

Line 21-25 "May the kingdom of justice come! May the Sikhs be united in love. May the hearts of the Sikhs be humble but their wisdom exalted — their wisdom in the keeping of the Lord, O Khalsa, say 'WAHEGURU' (wonderful Lord)."

Line 26 "Save us, O Father, from lust, wrath, greed, undue attachment and pride; and keep us always attached to Thy feet."

Line 31-33 "We offer this prayer in Thy presence. O WAHEGURU; Forgive us our sins. Help us in keeping ourselves pure. Bring us into the fellowship of only those men of love, in whose company we may remember Thy name."

Line 34-35 "Nanak, may Thy name forever be on the increase. And may everybody prosper by Thy grace".

in Ardas

SIKH CEREMONIES

Every important Sikh ceremony is performed in the presence of the Holy Granth. The ceremonies which are most important to a Sikh are:

NAMING CEREMONY

Sikhs name their children only after they are born, as it is customary to bring the child into the presence of the Holy Granth as soon as it is convenient and the mother is well enough to go to the Gurdwara. The Holy Granth is opened at random and an extract (Shabad) is read. Then the first letter of the 'Shabad' (hymn) on that page is chosen as the initial of the child's name. Now this could be any letter of the alphabet. For example if it is the letter (S) then any name such as Surinder, Surjit, Sukhdev, Satnam, Sarabjit, Satwant, Sukhwinder etc. could be chosen by the parents to their liking. Sometimes relatives and friends present also help by making suggestions. The selected name is then delcared by the officiating priest to all present. To this the word 'Singh' or 'Kaur' is added. 'Singh' is used for a boy and 'Kaur' for a girl. Literally 'Singh' means lion and 'Kaur' means princess. Now the full name could be Surinder Singh for a boy or Surinder Kaur for a girl and so on. Some Sikhs do not think it essential to add any family name or surname to their first full name, but most do.

Some of the most common Sikh surnames found in Britain are Bedi, Sodhi, Sahni, Kohli, Gill, Mann, Sidhu, Sandhu, Attwal, Sanghera, Bahra, Bhogal, Sahota, Cheema, Chahal, Mavi, Bansal, Sahota, Chhatwal, Grewal, Bajwa, Virdi, Ahluwallia, Nijhar and scores of others.

BAPTISM OR AMRIT

Baptism and marriage are the most important ceremonies in the life of a Sikh. It is in the form of a formal oath and initiation ceremony by which a Sikh becomes a true KHALSA (purified or chosen one) and like the Christian at confirmation acquires full membership of the Sikh brotherhood. As the ceremony culminates in the drinking of AMRIT (specially prepared holy water) so the term 'AMRIT DHARI SIKH' is often used. However, a Sikh should take AMRIT only when s/he is mature enough to realise the nature of the obligation s/he has chosen to accept.

AMRIT is Baptismal water which is prepared in an iron bowl by dissolving some PATASHAS or sugar cubes in water. The water is constantly stirred with a KHANDA (a small double-edged sword) and the GURBANNI (Holy verses) recited — which transform the sweet water into AMRIT (literally elixir). Part of this Amrit is taken through the mouth and the rest sprinkled sparingly on eyes, face and head.

Water, sugar cakes, double-edged sword and the bowl all symbolise something:

1. **WATER** — a symbol of life, cleanliness and purity as well as coolness and humanity.

2. **SUGAR CAKES** — easily soluble, symbolise the breakdown of social divisions and caste barriers as well as love and sweetness.

3. **'KHANDA'** — the double-edged steel sword is symbolic of strength, power,—single-mindedness and determination.

4. **'BAATA'** — the bowl symbolises the human mind where all the above virtues have taken a new shape.

5. **'BAANI'** — the holy verses purify the air, the breath and the soul.

MARRIAGE OR ANAND KAARJ

(ceremony of bliss) 'Anand Kaarj' literally means a good deed which is going to bring happiness and contentment. No Sikh marriage is regarded as truly complete unless the bride and groom present themselves before the Holy Granth and are blessed by the Guru, as well as by the congregation or the families present. A detailed account is given on another page.

THE DEATH CEREMONY

Usually, the ceremony is very simple. When a Sikh dies the body is first washed and new clothes put on. Then it is carried to the cremation ground in procession where appropriate prayers are said before the funeral pyre is lit by close relatives. In Britain a purpose-built crematorium is used. Later, the cooled ashes are collected and immersed into or 'presented to' natural running water — a river.

To complete the ceremony, then either in the home or in the Gurdwara, the daily reading of the Holy Granth begins. This takes about ten days. When all the 1430 pages have been read, the final service is held. Relatives and friends gather to join in the final prayers. The PARSHAD (holy food) is served and the people disperse. This marks the end of the period of mourning.

Members of the American Sikh Congregation with some Sikh religious leaders from Panjab (after receiving AMRIT at a special ceremony)

By courtesy Sikh Dharma Brotherhood (3HO Foundation)

SIKH MARRIAGES

As in many Eastern cultures, Sikh marriages are usually arranged. However, this word 'arranged' is not always properly understood and interpreted by people in Western Societies. Most British people consider marriage to be a private affair between two individuals who are marrying for love. But with Sikhs it is a matter which concerns two whole families as well, although the welfare and the wishes of the boy and girl are given due consideration.

An arranged marriage does not mean forcing a boy or a girl into a wedlock of parents choice only. It is agreeing to a marriage proposed by mutual discussion between the boy or the girl on one side and his or her parents and relatives on the other. This is in fact selecting the right partner from a number of choices or proposals.

However, depending upon the education and understanding of the individual family some boys and girls enjoy more freedom than others in choosing their life partners. Again, like 'courting', depending upon the boy's or the girl's individual character and personality, the amount of time spent on this procedure of 'selection and choice' may vary from a few weeks to many years.

The following criteria are usually adopted before making a marriage proposal:

a) The girl and the boy should not belong to the same village because 'children' of the same village are regarded as brothers and sisters living in the same community.

b) They should not be close relatives or have the same family name or surname; e.g. 'Smith' should not marry another 'Smith', Sidhu should not marry another Sidhu.

c) The two families should not have differing interests and social standings, so that they are able to co-operate with each other and thus help their children to make a success of their marriage.

d) The boy and the girl should not belong to different castes or sects, (although the Sikhs are instructed not to believe in a caste system, yet very few of them have felt inclined to disregard this particular rule).

e) The boy and the girl should not have anything on their record which could label him or her as immoral or criminal.

Nowadays, however, the most important factor before discussing a marriage proposal is the boy and the girl themselves, who usually show their willingness only after taking into account the educational standing and physical look of the proposed partner.

Usually, first photographs and then meetings are exchanged and again the whole family participates. However, the above criteria should not be taken as rigid rules; exceptions to the rule are as common as in any other society or religion.

"LIVING TOGETHER
DOES NOT MAKE HUSBAND & WIFE,

TRUE HUSBAND AND WIFE ARE THEY
WHO HAVE ONE SPIRIT IN TWO BODIES"

(The Holy Granth)

A SIKH WEDDING

"Thus, it is agreed that your son is our son and our daughter is your daughter."

The young man's first visit to the girl's house. Guess who serves him?

The betrothal ceremony in the boy's house or in the Gurdwara. His mouth is sweetened (or shut?) with a LADDOO by the girl's father. Lots of presents too.

Later, the boy's mother visits the girl's house and carries with her lots of presents for the would-be daughter-in-law. She places a gold ring on her finger.

Wedding day approaches. The groom and his party arrive at the bride's house or at the Gurdwara . . . and . . .

The 'MILNEE' takes place.

More guests arrive and are welcomed into the hall. Meanwhile . . . . .

the bridegroom waits patiently sitting in front of the Guru Granth . . . soon the bride arrives . . . escorted . . .

The Raagis play the music and sing holy verses. The priest then explains the obligations of marriage to both the bride and the groom, and asks for their approval. Then . . .

'LAAVAN' are read and sung.   The bridegroom leads the bride round the holy GURU GRANTH four times. The ceremony is almost over.

Time for a laugh and lunch.

Departure for in-laws' house. The bride and her family show emotions . . . lots of sobbing.

THE ANAND KAARJ
(Wedding Ceremony)

A Sikh wedding is called ANAND KAARJ meaning an act of bliss. Sometime before the wedding day another important ceremony called 'KURMAAYEE' or 'SHAGN' takes place usually at the bridgegroom's house or the Gurdwara. It is a formal engagement ceremony involving a promise to marry and an exchange of rings and other presents. But the word 'Kurmaayee' literally means the 'coming' or the meeting of the parents of both the boy and the girl, and this shows the importance attached to the 'union' of the two families.

The proper wedding ceremony (Anand Kaarj) takes place usually at the bride's house or the Gurdwara. On this occasion the parents of the bride act as hosts. As soon as the marriage party (consisting of the bridegroom, his parents, relatives and friends) arrive, the 'MILNEE' is performed. Again the word 'milnee' means the 'meeting' of especially fathers and nearest paternal and maternal relatives of the bride and groom. For example the maternal uncle of the bride comes forward carrying a token present for the maternal uncle of the bridegroom.

After a formal exchange of greetings and handing over the presents, they usually embrace each other showing mutual respect and affection. Although the bridegroom remains the centre of attraction, his participation in this ceremony is no more than a silent spectator.

When the important near relatives have done the 'milnee' the whole party take some refreshments which have been kept ready to be served. By now the time is approximately ten o'clock.

After refreshments, the bridegroom (usually carrying a sword and saffron-coloured scarf) leads the party into DARBAR-SAHIB (the congregation-hall) where the Holy Granth is present. He sits in front of the Guru Granth and waits for the bride to arrive. In the meantime RAAGIS (Sikh musicians of the holy word) sing and play the sacred music. Then the bride enters the hall, escorted by one or more sisters or sister-in-law or any other near relative or friend. She wears a deep red SALWAR, KAMEEZ and DUPATTA which are usually richly embroidered in gold. Her face almost veiled by the 'dupatta', she sits down next to the groom. They silently listen to the music.

Soon the priest gives them a brief talk about the 'union of two bodies to make one soul' and explains to them the importance of obligations or duties towards each other for the rest of their lives. The bride and the groom then vow to accept the duties of marriage by bowing before the Holy Granth.

After this formal acceptance of each other in the presence of the congregation, the bride's father then hands over one end of the groom's scarf to the bride, while the other end is held by the groom. This indicates that the father is giving his daughter away.

Now the most important part of the ceremony begins. This is called LAAVAN*. The GRANTHI — one who is proficient in reading the Granth — reads a marriage verse (a Laav). At the end of it the Raagis begin to sing the same verse, while both the bride and groom stand up and, led by the groom, walk gently round the Holy Granth to complete one circle. They bow and sit. The second verse is then read and they walk another circle. Then the four verses are read and the four journeys are made. The whole ceremony is concluded by the singing of the final hymn called ANAND, and the ARDAS (prayer) is said. After this KARRAH PARSHAD (sacred food) is served and at the same time the guests flock to the bride and groom to bless them, congratulate them and present them with cash or gifts according to their ability and attachment to the family. The time is well past twelve now, and there is a reception ready somewhere at a restaurant, hotel or hall.

---

*LAAVAN (Literally, putting or joining together — i.e. the bride and the groom are joined together internally by the holy word or verse and externally by the symbolic scarf). Here this 'union' takes place by a formal act of going round the Holy Granth, four times clockwise.

THE BRIDEGROOM AND THE BRIDE

LAAVAN — the bride and groom walking round the Holy Granth during the ceremony.

A GURDWARA (SIKH PLACE OF WORSHIP)

In the Gurdwara, before entering the DARBAR SAHIB (hall, where the holy book Guru Granth is placed) people must cover their heads and take off their shoes. Visitors without a proper head cover, i.e. turban or chunni (lady's scarf) can borrow scarves provided by the Gurdwara, or otherwise a large handkerchief could serve the purpose. Shoes should be left in the racks.

On approaching the Guru Granth Sahib (Holy Book), Sikhs usually put some money on the holy cloth or into the GOLAK (donation-box). Some, especially women, bring articles of food such as milk, sugar and butter which are then collected for the LANGAR (free kitchen).

It is obligatory for every Sikh, young and old, to show the utmost respect to the Guru Granth. So, as soon as they come face to face with the Holy Granth they bow down on their knees, most touching their foreheads to the floor.

In the congregation women sit, generally, on one side and the men on the other side of the hall. It is rude and disrespectful to show one's back or stretch one's feet towards the Holy Granth. That is why everyone tries to sit cross-legged. Also it is customary that everyone sits on the carpeted floor, which is symbolic of down-to-earth humility before the Guru and equality with fellow Sikhs.

On one side of the MANJI SAHIB (Guru's seat) RAAGIS (musicians) recite SHABADS (hymns) and play the harmonium and TABLA (a pair of small seated drums). Occasionally they stop reciting and one of them elaborates on the Guru's word (hymns) and his teachings. Sometimes they choose to sing an incident from Sikh history and talk about it. Finally, the service ends with ARDAS (formal prayer).

Everyone stands up, bows heads and folds hands showing humility and submission to the Guru and the WAHEGURU (God Himself). When the priest says ARDAS, he occasionally interrupts it with the word 'Waheguru' (like Amen in English). Finally, 'PARSHAD' (warm sweet food made of flour, purified butter, sugar and water) is served, before the congregation leaves.

THE LANGAR
The institution of 'Langar' is an important aspect of the Sikh way of life. 'Langar' literally means kitchen. But in Sikh terminology, langar in the Gurdwara means the cooking and serving of food on a large scale. There is always a queue of willing helpers to do this service and the food is free to every visitor — Sikh and non Sikh alike.

This practice also serves as a practical demonstration and a reminder to the Sikhs that they should not believe in the caste system, and should eat together irrespective of their status, high or low, rich or poor. However, the food served at the Gurdwara is always vegetarian. In Britain special congregation services are held on either Saturday or Sunday and the 'Langar' is an almost inseparable part of the whole service.

GURDWARA—
TAKHAT SRI
KESH GARH SAHIB
at Anandpur Sahib

A SIKH CONGREGATION

SHABAD KEERTAN (Singing of the holy word)

MUSIC and MUSICAL INSTRUMENTS

The Sikhs' love of music is no less than any other community's. However, the music which is commonly associated with the Sikhs can be described as —

A. Sacred or Devotional Music:

This is a traditional style of singing SHABADS and is popularly known as GURBANI SANGEET, or SHABAD KEERTAN. Shabad is an independent hymn or extract from the Holy Granth which is sung by RAAGIS conforming as far as possible to the style and tone set in the Granth. Generally, a party of three RAAGIS performs Shabad Keertan, each playing a musical instrument. One plays the JORRI (tabla) and leaves the singing to the other two except to augment the volume at appropriate phrases. The other two play the BAJA (harmoniums) and sing in duet. Professional or experienced RAAGIS manage to create a rare tranquil and spiritual atmosphere in the Gurdwara.

THE BAJA (Harmonium) It is the most common and the most important musical instrument of the Sikhs. It has a keyboard rather like a piano, and even a child can play it. It does not cost much and can be carried easily because of its small size (approximately 2' x 1' x 1'). In Panjabi terminology any instrument which produces a musical note by blowing or puffing of air is called Baja.

JORRI (Tabla) Jorri literally means 'pair'. These are two one-sided drums, one narrower than the other, made of hollowed wood and the surface made of quality skin usually from goats. Both drums are played by hands; the narrower top is played with the fingers only while the broad top is played with different parts of the hand — the finger-tips, the lower hard part of the palm and the whole open palm. Both the harmonium and the tabla can be used for any kind of Indian music from classical to folk music.

B. Ballad Singing

Stories of heroic deeds from Sikh history are sung by DHAADIS (Ballad Singers) which consist of a party of three to four persons. Two of them play the DHADS as they sing alternately couplets and duets, and one of them plays the SARANGI. They all remain standing throughout their musical discourse. This type of music is still very popular with the general public although almost confined to the Gurdwara or other open gatherings celebrating a religious festival or fair.

DHAD This is a small two-sided hand drum with a thin waist. A cloth band is tied round this thin waist which helps the DHAADI to hold the DHAD firmly in one hand while he taps (plays) it hard with fingers of the other hand. (See picture on page 59)

SARANGI This is a stringed wooden instrument which is played with a bow. There are four main strings but beneath them there are as many as forty complementary strings, which add to the effect and volume of the sound. (See picture on page 59)

C. Folk Music

Folk Music is extremely popular and the most important single source of entertainment in the Panjab — the homeland of the Sikhs. It is performed in various forms — from light singing to vigorous dancing. The most popular of them are BHANGRA and GIDHA.

BHANGRA is the most popular Panjabi dance which is known for its vigour and speed. As such a lot of energy and stamina is required to perform this dance for even a few minutes, Bhangra is a collective dance and the participants are usually men dressed in loose colourful uniform. Women can join in equally. Similarly a Bhangra party may consist of any number of persons, usually more than six, at least one of them playing the **DHOLE** (a large two-sided drum) which sets the tone and the speed of the dance. Sometimes Bhangra troupes also use other minor instruments as well as some folk songs during their performance.

GIDHA, like Bhangra, is also a very energetic and impressive Panjabi dance, but is almost exclusively performed by women. The musical instrument used on such occasions is called the **DHOLAK**. Like Dhole, it is a hollow wooden cylinder, slightly bulging out in the middle, with parchment on both sides.

IK-TARA is yet another popular Panjabi musical instrument for accompanying folklore and pop songs. Ik-tara literally means 'one string'. It consists of a small flat dried pumpkin covered with parchment. Only one finger is used to play this instrument.

BAJA (HARMONIUM)

JORRI (TABLA)

American Sikh musicians sing English translations of the Guru's words.

By courtesy Sikh Dharma (3HO Foundation)

54

A SACRED HYMN

1. Ex - tend thy hand to shield me Lord, And all my hearts de - sires ful - fil. Ever may my mind dwell at Thy feet. Deem me Thy own and work Thy weal.

2. Slay Thou my ene - mies one and all, Save me from them by Thy own hand. May all the peo - ple live in peace, who serve and do as I com - mand.

3. "May Thine own hand be ever my shield,
   and all my foes forthwith destroy.
   May all my hopes fulfillment find,
   ever may I crave rapport with Thee.

4. I may not worship other than Thee,
   when Thou canst grant me every boon.
   Keep my disciples from all harm,
   and crush my enemies one by one.

5. Uphold me with Thine own strength,
   fear of the hour of death annul.
   Be ever Thou on my side O Lord,
   and take me under Thy banner of steel."

(Guru Gobind Singh)

(ਬੇਨਤੀ ਚੌਪਈ ॥ ਪਾਤਸ਼ਾਹੀ ੧੦)

1. ਹਮਰੀ ਕਰੋ ਹਾਥ ਦੈ ਰੱਛਾ ॥ ਪੂਰਨ ਹੋਇ ਚਿਤ ਕੀ ਇੱਛਾ ॥
   ਤਵ ਚਰਨਨ ਮਨ ਰਹੈ ਹਮਾਰਾ ॥ ਅਪਨਾ ਜਾਨ ਕਰੋ ਪ੍ਰਤਿਪਾਰਾ ॥

2. ਹਮਰੇ ਦੁਸਟ ਸਭੈ ਤੁਮ ਘਾਵਹੁ ॥ ਆਪੁ ਹਾਥ ਦੈ ਮੋਹਿ ਬਚਾਵਹੁ ॥
   ਸੁਖੀ ਬਸੈ ਮੋਰੋ ਪਰਿਵਾਰਾ ॥ ਸੇਵਕ ਸਿਖ ਸਭੈ ਕਰਤਾਰਾ ॥

3. ਮੋ ਰੱਛਾ ਨਿਜ ਕਰ ਦੈ ਕਰੀਐ ॥ ਸਭ ਬੈਰਨ ਕੋ ਆਜ ਸੰਘਰੀਐ ॥
   ਪੂਰਨ ਹੋਇ ਹਮਾਰੀ ਆਸਾ ॥ ਤੋਰ ਭਜਨ ਕੀ ਰਹੈ ਪਿਆਸਾ ॥

4. ਤੁਮਹਿ ਛਾਡਿ ਕੋਈ ਅਵਰ ਨ ਧਿਆਊਂ ॥ ਜੋ ਬਰ ਚਾਹੋਂ ਸੁ ਤੁਮ ਤੇ ਪਾਊਂ ॥
   ਸੇਵਕ ਸਿਖ ਹਮਾਰੇ ਤਾਰੀਅਹਿ ॥ ਚੁਨਿ ਚੁਨਿ ਸਤ੍ਰ ਹਮਾਰੇ ਮਾਰੀਅਹਿ ॥

5. ਆਪੁ ਹਾਥ ਦੈ ਮੁਝੈ ਉਬਰਿਐ ॥ ਮਰਨ ਕਾਲ ਕਾ ਤ੍ਰਾਸ ਨਿਵਰਿਐ ॥
   ਹੂਜੋ ਸਦਾ ਹਮਾਰੇ ਪੱਛਾ ॥ ਸ੍ਰੀ ਅਸਿਧੁਜ ਜੂ ਕਰਿਅਹੁ ਰੱਛਾ ॥

56

↑

SCENES OF PANJABI GIDHA

↓

By courtesy Des Perdes

on the village common ↑

on the English stage ↓

THE DHAADEES
(ballad singers)

← **in traditional dress**

AND

in western style

↓

THE CENTRAL SIKH MUSEUM
&
ENTRANCE TO THE DARBAR SAHIB
AMRITSAR

Sikh art and architecture is original as well as incorporating some of the best features of Hindu and Muslim Art in India. Some of the famous names associated with the Sikh School of Art are S. Kehar Singh, Bhai Kishan Singh and Bishan Singh, Amrita Shergill, S. Thakar Singh, Giani Gian Singh, Sardar Sobha Singh and S. Kirpal Singh.

That Sikh art and architecture originated and flourished noticeably in the first half of the 19th century may be attributed to Maharaja Ranjit Singh's rule in Panjab (1797–1839). A fine example of this art is found in the decorative panelling of the Harmander, known as Golden Temple, in Amritsar. Similarly, many paintings belonging to this period may be found in the central Sikh Museum which is situated within the Golden Temple complex*. Most of the oil and fresco paintings depict various events and scenes from Sikh history.

The design and decor of the Harmander Sahib (Golden Temple) are an outstanding example of Sikh art and architecture. As well as the frescoes, Sikh workmen have really excelled in presenting on the temple's walls a rare harmony of brass and gilded copper studded with small pieces of precious stones. "Among its typical features are a multiplicity of kiosks which ornament the parapets, angles, and every prominence and projection, the invariable use of the fluted dome generally covered with copper gilded with gold or brass . . . no one can fail to be attracted by their animated and picturesque appearance." (P. Brown)

*Sikhs are particularly unfortunate to have lost the treasure of their rich heritage of works of art and literature twice. First during the evacuation of Anandpur by Guru Gobind Singh, and again through destruction by fire of the Sikh Reference library during 'Operation Blue Star' in June 1984, when many buildings within the Golden Temple complex were destroyed by the Indian Army.

SRI HARMANDER SAHIB (also known as Golden Temple)
at Amritsar — the holy city of the Sikhs

HARMANDER is the original name of the 'Golden Temple'. (HAR means Lord and MANDER means temple — Lord's Temple). The central dome and the upper half of its walls are covered with gold leaf, hence the name Golden Temple. It is a two storied marble building standing on a 67 x 67 ft. platform in the centre of the sacred pool called Amritsar. ('Amrit' means nector or the elixir of life and 'sar' means pool or tank). The central structure itself is 40.5 ft square and has a door on each side. The four doors, on each of the north, south, east and west sides are symbolic, to point out that the Harmander is open to all people from all directions, irrespective of their caste, creed, colour or sex. A twenty-foot marble causeway on the western side of the pool leads to the Harmander. A 38-foot-wide promenade called the 'Parikarma' runs round the pool. Further beyond, surrounding the parikarma are rows of 'varandhas' and restrooms for the pilgrims, and also for officials looking after the place.

With the exception of the words HARMANDER and the Golden Temple used as proper nouns, a Sikh place of worship should, essentially, be called a GURDWARA — not Sikh temple. The word temple or mander generally refers to the Hindu place of worship where idols of Gods and Goddesses are normally seen and worshipped, which is not a Sikh practice.

The use of the name Sikh Temple for many Gurdwaras in Britain and Canada is partly due to ignorance and partly because of lack of effort by many Sikhs in popularising the word Gurdwara in western countries, especially among non-Sikhs.

THE AKAL TAKHAT

The original building which was destroyed
by the Indian army in June 1984

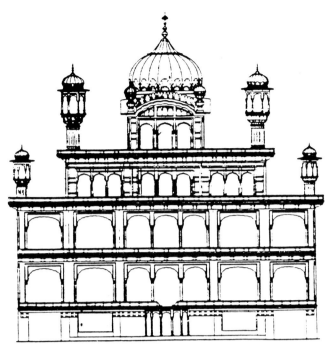

(Front elevation of the rebuilt Akal Takhat
which rose like a phoenix after its destruction.

Literally 'Akal' means timeless, which to Sikhs means the Timeless, the Immortal,The God — and since 'Takhat' means throne, the name Akal Takhat means the 'Throne of the Immortal' or the 'Throne Divine'.

Within ten years of the completion of Harmander (the name Golden Temple became popular later) and after the persecution and death of the fifth Guru Arjan, the idea of such an institution as Akal Takhat was conceived by the sixth Guru Hargobind, and the first building was completed in 1609. Both these buildings faced each other; Harmander became the spiritual centre for Sikh pilgrims, and the Akal Takhat began to be looked upon as a symbol of temporal authority for the whole Sikh world. The present building of Akal Takhat is a majestic four storied structure 77 ft x 51 ft at its base, and it may be aptly described as the nerve centre of the Sikhs and Sikhism.

The importance of the institution of Akal Takhat explains why the Sikh community felt so bitter and upset, and reacted so strongly when the Indian army attacked and almost demolished this building with cannon fire in June 1984.

It is the Akal Takhat which is the real HOME or resting place of the most sacred and original copy of the Sikh Scriptures — the Adi Granth or Guru Granth. It is from here that every morning (5 a.m. in winter and 4 a.m. in summer) the Guru Granth is carried in a golden 'Palakee' (Palanquin) to the Harmander (Golden Temple) and then carried back to the Akal Takhat's care at 10 p.m. in winter and 11 p.m. in summer — thus the designation of the Akal Takhat is as the guardian or the custodian of the Sikh faith.

The Akal Takhat is regarded as the highest or the supreme court of the Sikhs. It is here that important 'Gurmatas' (decisions) regarding the Sikhs and Sikhism are made in the presence of the assembled Khalsa. It is from here that the high priest of the Akal Takhat (and not of the Golden Temple) makes his pronouncements (HUKAMNAMA), and issues directions on matters of extreme importance to the Sikhs, which are regarded as a binding law for the whole Sikh nation.

Thus, to the Sikhs, the importance of the Akal Takhat is both Spiritual and Temporal, whereas that of the 'Golden Temple' is purely spiritual. Also, it is for this reason that the Akal Takhat is the only Sikh shrine where two huge flagpoles stand side by side, one bearing the flag of 'MEEREE' (Temporal Authority) and the other the flag of 'PEEREE' (Spiritual Authority).

NANAK JHIRA BIDAR

DARBAR SAHIB, TARN TARAN

CHAMKAUR SAHIB

DERA BABA NANAK

AN EXAMPLE OF ART INSIDE THE HARMANDER (Golden Temple)

WORK ON WHITE MARBLE

MORE SPECIMENS OF SIKH ART

AMRITSAR — the holy city

Extracts from some of the letters received by the SGPC* (from non-Sikh Indians in high office) on the occasion of the 400th anniversary of the founding of Amritsar.

Amritsar has been associated with both the spiritual and the national upliftment of India. 400 years is not a long span in terms of history. But the 400 years of Amritsar have given it a uniqueness in Indian history as a spiritual centre of Sikh religion . . . . Amritsar lives up to its glorious past. The spirit of sacrifice will always give inspiration to humanity for resisting injustice and for fighting for human dignity and righteousness in the world.

CHANDRA SHEKHAR — M.P. (President, Janta Party) September 17, 1977

Celebration of the 400th anniversary of the foundation of Amritsar is an occasion of great historical significance not only for the Sikh community but for the entire country . . . . . . While the Golden Temple is a nerve-centre of Sikh cultural and religious traditions and a place of spiritual solace for all Indians,* the Jallianwala Bagh symbolizes the indomitable spirit of India rising against the forces of imperialism and injustice.

(S.M. ABDULLAH) — Chief Minister Jammu and Kashmir September 26, 1977

This beautiful city of AMRITSAR, founded by Guru Ram Das 400 years ago, occupies a unique place in the history of India. Besides being the holiest of the Sikh Shrines with Golden Temple, the part it played in the Independence struggle needs no explanation here. . . I am sure the history of Amritsar will remain a perennial source of inspiration to coming generations that no price paid is too high for Freedom.

GEORGE FERNANDES — Minister of Industry, India September 22, 1977

The historic city of Amritsar . . . has . . . had the distinction of being in the forefront of the country's freedom struggle and has witnessed the bloodbath of Jallianwala when hundreds of its citizens were gunned down by the imperialist troops in their vain bid to crush the freedom-loving urge of the valiant Panjabis.

L.K. JHA — Governor, Jammu & Kashmir, September 24, 1977

---

*see page 90

PANJABI LANGUAGE

Panjabi is one of the major languages of the Indian sub-continent, and is spoken by well over sixty million people. In England and Canada, it is the 'Home Language' (mother tongue) of the majority of Asians from the sub-continent.

The Panjabi alphabet consists of 35 characters (letters) written like English from left to right. The order of the alphabet is arranged in seven groups of five letters each, and most of it is based on well defined phonetic sound patterns — as below.

However, apart from the first three letters of the Panjabi alphabet, which represent five English vowels, there are nine vowel signs —

ਕਾਰ	ਦਿਲ	ਫ਼ੀਲ	ਫੁਲ	ਫੂਲ	ਫੇਟ	ਫੈਟ	ਨੋਟ	ਨੌਟ
car	fill	feel	full	fool	fate	fat	note	not (naught)

Once the alphabet and its nine vowel signs have been mastered, learning to read and write Panjabi can be achieved quickly and fairly accurately. This is because Panjabi letters produce only one distinctive sound — unlike English and z, g and j, c and k etc. Similar is the case with vowel signs.

Learning to write Panjabi letters can be easy if practised in groups of similar pattern, as shown below —

| ਪ, ਖ, ਧ, ਜ, ਬ, ਬ, ਘ | (The 'u' pattern) |

| ਟ, ੲ, ੲ, ੲ, ਦ, ੲ, ੲ, ੲ | (opposite of '5' pattern) |

| ਤ, ੜ, ੜ, ੜ, ੳ, ੜ, ੜ | (fig 3 pattern) |

| ਹ, ਰ, ਗਾ, ਕ | ਨ, ਠ, ਲ, ਫ | ਮ, ਸ, ਜ, ਚ, ਅ |

69

THE PANJABI SCRIPT

The Panjabi script has often been referred to as 'Gurmukhi' because of the popular (but mistaken) belief that it had been invented by the second Sikh Guru, Guru Angad - which is wrong. In fact this script was the one introduced to Guru Nanak (the founder of Sikhism) when he first went to school at the age of six. However, a major contribution to Panjabi which the early Sikh Gurus did make was their popularisation of the indigenous script by adopting it for a written record of their holy verses.

The word GURMUKHI is a compound form of GURU+ MUKH. Mukh in Panjabi means 'face' or 'mouth' so the word Gurmukhi means 'like the Guru's face' or 'from the Guru's mouth'. Again, since Panjabi letters are neither like the Guru's face nor do they come from the Guru's mouth, it is inappropriate to call them Gurmukhi.

However, the word 'Gurmukhi' has been correctly used and understood for the 'holy utterances' of the Gurus which have been written down and compiled into a holy book called Guru Granth (Sikh scriptures).

No word, verse or piece of writing in Panjabi can or should be called Gurmukhi unless it belongs to the Guru's original verses. Gurmukhi is indeed another word for 'Gurbani' (Guru's holy utterances) which are now transposed into print.

Thus, like the name of the land, people and language, this same word Panjabi is the only appropriate word for naming the indigenous script of this language - and hence Panjabi script.

ਕੀ ਅਸੀਂ ਕਦੀ ਸੋਚਿਆ ਹੈ ?

(specimen of written Panjabi)

1. ਸਿੱਖ ਕੌਮ ਦੀ ਮਾਂ-ਬੋਲੀ ਪੰਜਾਬੀ ਹੈ ।
2. ਕਿਸੇ ਵੀ ਕੌਮ ਦੀ ਬੋਲੀ ਉਸ ਕੌਮ ਦੇ ਸਵਾਸ ਹੁੰਦੇ ਹਨ ।
3. ਕਿਸੇ ਵੀ ਕੌਮ ਨੂੰ ਖਤਮ ਕਰਨ ਲਈ ਗੋਲੀ ਜਾਂ ਤਲਵਾਰ ਦੀ ਲੋੜ ਨਹੀਂ, ਸਗੋਂ ਉਸ ਕੌਮ ਦੀ ਬੋਲੀ ਨੂੰ ਖਤਮ ਕਰਨਾ ਹੀ ਕਾਫੀ ਹੈ ।
4. ਜੋ ਲੋਕ ਆਪਣੀ ਬੋਲੀ, ਆਪਣੇ ਧਰਮ ਅਤੇ ਸਭਿਆਚਾਰ ਦੀ ਖੁਦ ਹੀ ਕਦਰ ਨਹੀਂ ਕਰਦੇ, ਉਹ ਦੂਜੀਆਂ ਕੌਮਾਂ ਦੇ ਲੋਕਾਂ ਕੋਲੋਂ ਕੀ ਆਸ ਰਖ ਸਕਦੇ ਹਨ ।
5. ਪ੍ਰਦੇਸਾਂ ਵਿਚ ਜੰਮਦੇ, ਪਲਦੇ ਸਿੱਖ ਬੱਚੇ ਆਪਣੀ ਕੌਮੀ ਬੋਲੀ ਪੰਜਾਬੀ ਨੂੰ ਲਿਖਣ ਬੋਲਣ ਵਿਚ ਕਿਉਂ ਪਿੱਛੇ ਹਨ । ਇਸ ਵਿਚ ਕਸੂਰ ਬੱਚਿਆਂ ਦਾ ਹੈ ਜਾਂ ਮਾਪਿਆਂ ਦਾ ?
6. ਕੀ ਅਸੀਂ ਕਦੀ ਆਪਣੇ ਬੱਚੇ ਨੂੰ ਪੰਜਾਬੀ ਸਿਖਾਉਣ ਬਾਰੇ ਗੰਭੀਰਤਾ ਨਾਲ ਸੋਚਿਆ ਹੈ ?
7. ਕੀ ਅਸੀਂ ਕਦੀ ਆਪਣੇ ਬੱਚੇ ਨੂੰ ਪੰਜਾਬੀ ਲਿਖਣ ਪੜਨ ਲਈ ਪ੍ਰੇਰਿਆ ਹੈ ?
8. ਕੀ ਅਸੀਂ ਕਦੀ ਆਪਣੇ ਬੱਚੇ ਦੇ ਸਕੂਲ ਵਿਚ ਪੰਜਾਬੀ ਪੜਨ ਸੰਬੰਧੀ ਕੋਈ ਪੁੱਛ ਗਿੱਛ ਕੀਤੀ ਹੈ ?
9. ਕੀ ਅਸੀਂ ਕਦੀ ਇਹ ਜਾਨਣ ਦੀ ਕੋਸ਼ਿਸ਼ ਕੀਤੀ ਹੈ ਕਿ ਪੰਜਾਬੀ ਵਿਚ G.C.S.E. ਆਦਿ 'ਚ ਇਮਤਿਹਾਨ ਪਾਸ ਕਰਨ ਨਾਲ ਕੀ ਕੀ ਫਾਇਦੇ ਹੋ ਸਕਦੇ ਹਨ ?
10. ਕੀ ਅਸੀਂ ਅਜੇ ਵੀ ਆਪਣੀ ਕੌਮੀ ਬੋਲੀ ਨੂੰ ਇਕ ਬੇਲੋੜੀ ਜ਼ਬਾਨ ਸਮਝੀ ਜਾ ਰਹੇ ਹਾਂ ?
11. ਆਪਣੇ ਬੱਚਿਆਂ ਨੂੰ ਉਹਨਾਂ ਦੇ ਅਗਲੇ ਵਿਰਸੇ ਤੋਂ ਦੂਰ ਲਿਜਾਣ ਦਾ ਜ਼ੁੰਮੇਵਾਰ ਕੌਣ ਹੈ ?
12. ਕੀ ਅਸੀਂ ਆਪਣੇ ਪਿਛੋਕੜ ਦੇ ਦੇਸ, ਆਪਣੇ ਧਰਮ, ਬੋਲੀ ਜਾਂ ਸਭਿਆਚਾਰ ਵਿਚ ਕੋਈ ਵੀ ਮਾਣ ਵਾਲੀ ਗਲ ਨਹੀਂ ਵੇਖ ਸਕਦੇ?
13. ਕੀ ਅਸੀਂ ਕਦੀ ਸੋਚਿਆ ਹੈ ਕਿ ਪ੍ਰਦੇਸਾਂ ਵਿਚ ਪੈਸਾ ਕਮਾਉਣ ਦੇ ਨਾਲ ਆਪਣੀ ਔਲਾਦ ਗਵਾਉਣ ਤੋਂ ਕਿਵੇਂ ਬਚ ਸਕਦੇ ਹਾਂ ?
14. ਚੇਤੇ ਰਖੋ ! ਦੂਜੀਆਂ ਕੌਮਾਂ ਦੇ ਲੋਕ ਸਾਡੀ ਇੱਜ਼ਤ ਤਾਂ ਹੀ ਕਰਨਗੇ ਜੇਕਰ ਪਹਿਲਾਂ ਅਸੀਂ ਖੁਦ ਆਪਣੀ ਇੱਜ਼ਤ ਆਪ ਕਰਨੀ ਸਿਖਾਂਗੇ ।

DR. (BHAI) VIR SINGH

Bhai Vir Singh is the most respected and noble Sikh of the 20th century. He was born in 1872 and died at the age of 85 in 1957. Vir Singh's contribution to Panjabi Language and Literature can be easily and aptly compared to Shakespeare's work in English.

Not only was he an outstanding writer, a poet, a novelist and a critic, but also a great theologian who dedicated himself to the task of expounding Sikh history and philosophy for more than fifty years of his life.

Because of the nature of his services in various fields, he was awarded:

i)   the title of 'Bhai' by the supreme religious authority of the Sikhs at Amritsar.

ii) 'Padma Bhushan' (one of the highest honours in literature) by the Government of India, and the 'SAHITYA AKADAMY' award.

iii) an Honorary Doctorate by the University of the Panjab. One commentator once called him the "sixth river in the land of the five rivers."

THE SIKH HOMELAND

JAMMU & KASHMIR

Pathankot

GURDASPUR

HIMACHAL

Dhera Baba Nanak

Qadian

Dasuya

Ajnala

Batala

Har-Gobindpur

AMRITSAR

Beas

Wagha

HOSHIARPUR

PAKISTAN

Tarn Tarn

Kartarpur

Goindwal

Kapurthala

JULUNDHER

ANANDPUR-SAHIB

Khemkaran

Sultanpur

Phagwara

Harike-Pattan

Nakodar

Phillaur

Nawanshahar

ROPAR

Machhiwara

LUDHIANA

Chamkaur Sahib

FEROZEPUR

Jagraon

Doraha

Morinda

CHANDIGARH

FARIDKOT

Moga

Rai Kote

Khanna

Kharar

Jlalabad

Dina.Kangar

Fatehgarh Sahib

Muktsar

Kot-Kapura

SIRHIND

Fazilka

P A N J A B

Malerkotla

Rajpura

Malaut

Dhuri

PATIALA

Ambala

Barnala

Nabha

Abohar

BATHINDA

SANGRUR

Damdama Sahib

Mansa

Khanauri

HARYANA

RAJASTHAN

100 KILOMETRES

SIKH FOODS

Sikhs prefer to eat wheat rather than rice, and very few of them are strictly vegetarian. Wheat is their staple diet. They may eat any meat. However, Sikhs avoid eating beef out of consideration for Hindu feelings with whom they share many things. Similarly, they would avoid eating pork when they are in the company of Muslims. As Sikhs do not believe in rituals, they do not accept meat which is prepared by a ritual killing of the animal.

Like many other communities in the world, the Sikhs take great pride in their food and their cooking skills. Children learn to cook when they are young and try to perfect this art before they are married. Many Sikh women reflect unkindly on the mother whose daughter is not expert in cooking various dishes without any help from notes and recipe books. Many Indian cookery books on the market are written mainly for the benefit of non—Indians.

Some of the most common names in Sikh meals are —

A.   **ROTI or PHULKA:** The Roti is made from wholemeal or brown wheat flour and is fairly simple to make. It is flat and round, approximately six inches in diameter and looks like a pancake. The Phulka is a finer version of Roti and is named as such because it bubbles or puffs up like a saucer-shaped balloon. Chapatti is another name for Roti or Phulka and is not very popular in Panjabi homes, especially among the Sikhs. PURI is yet another type of Roti, which is smaller in size and is deep fried like potato chips.

      PARAUTHA: A richer and more nourishing form of roti is called parautha. It is made by folding and rolling the dough a number of times with or without fillings, and is fried in ghee, margarine or vegetable oil. It needs an expert to make a really good parautha. It is the most popular morning snack and is less likely to be eaten in the afternoon or evening.

B.   **SABZI and DAAL:** Whether vegetarian or non-vegetarian, no meal in a Sikh family is complete without either a SABZI (cooked vegetable) or DAAL (cooked pulse) and indeed both.

      This is one area where Indian cooking is difficult to match, not only in the variety of Daals and Sabzees but also in their cooking methods. Pulses, which come in different colours and size, are amongst the most popular dishes because they are cheap, easy to cook, tasty and nutritious.

      Some of the most common names in this group are —

      (i) SABZI — cauliflower, cabbage, lady-fingers (Okra), aubergine, peas, green pepper, potato, carrot, turnip, gourd (bitter), spinach.

      (ii) DAAL — Chana or Chholay (gram or chick peas), moong (green lentil), mansoor (red or yellow lentils), mah or urad (black lentil) etc.

      (iii) SAAG — a kind of cooked puree, mainly from green mustard.

      (iv) **DAHI or YOGURT:** an important complementary item to the Panjabi meal and usually enriched with other ingredients before serving.

      (v) **PANEER:** (specially prepared cheese cubes) when cooked is more tender and tasty than veal and is the most popular vegetarian diet.

C.   **SNACKS and SWEETS:** As far as snacks and sweet dishes are concerned Indian cooking is hard to beat. Although the serving of a dessert after a full meal is not regarded as important, a sweet dish like Kheer (rice pudding) is often served as part of the meal.

      Many Indian sweets are made of milk, sugar, gram flour and ghee. Some of the popular ones are — RASGULLA, GULAB JAMAN, BARFI, LADDOO, JALLEBI, HALWA, GAJERELLA, DOODH BARE etc.

Among the snacks the most common ones are PAKORRAS (spicy savoury snack) which are quick and simple to make, and there are scores of varieties of Pakorras from vegetarian to non-vegetarian. Similarly SAMOSAS (triangular shaped pastry envelopes with fillings ranging from various vegetables to minced meat) are very popular but are rather expensive to make.

A PANJABI RECIPE

PAKORRA — KARHI: This dish is a very good substitute for Daal and Sabzi for the main meal, but very few Indian cookery books mention it. Actually it needs two separate recipes and to be cooked separately, and finally mixed to make one dish.

For Pakorras

Ingredients:
8 oz gramflour
1 teaspoon salt
½　　"　　coriander
½　　"　　red chilli
½　　"　　ground ginger
1 pinch of ground cummin
Water to mix
Oil for frying
Sliced vegetable, (usually potatoes,
　　cauliflower, onion, aubergine)

For Karhi

4 oz gramflour
8 oz yoghurt
2-3 medium-size chopped onions
Some sliced root ginger, garlic, green chillies.
2 teaspoons salt
1　　"　　turmeric powder
Some cooking oil

Method

Sieve all dry ingredients into a good size bowl and add sufficient water to make a thick batter mixture. Cover each vegetable slice with a liberal coat of batter mixture and dip it into deep, hot oil in a frying pan. Cook till golden brown. You need only 8 - 12 Pakorras for the Karhi, use the rest as snacks.

In a good size pan fry onion, ginger, garlic, and add chillies, salt and turmeric till golden brown. In another container mix gramflour and yoghurt to make a thick mixture, and then pour this mixture into the other cooked ingredients, add sufficient water and keep stirring until it starts simmering. Cook for another ½ hour on low heat, then add 8-12 Pakorras and leave for another 15 minutes.

Serve with Phulka or Rice.

SOME STORIES FROM THE LIFE OF GURU NANAK ⟶

WHICH FOOD

During his travels within the Panjab, one day Nanak reached a large village which is now called Eminabad. His friend Mardana was with him. They were both tired and hungry and wanted to have some rest and food. Although he had never met him, Nanak knew that there was a certain person in the village named Lalo, who was an extremely humble and honest man. He was a so-called low-caste carpenter and earned his living honestly by working hard all day. Nanak went straight to his little one-roomed house and asked for food. Lalo too had heard about Nanak, who did not believe in caste or class, and he had once wished to visit this holy man. But he had never thought or imagined that this holy man would one day come to his house himself and even ask for food.

When Lalo saw the Guru, first he did not believe his eyes. He was so stunned that he even forgot to ask the Guru to come in. But as soon as the Guru touched him and spoke to him he welcomed the Guru into his small room with great respect and care.

In the same village lived another man, named Malik Bhago. He was a high caste Hindu (Brahmin) and was the head man of the village. He was rich and had acquired his wealth by wicked means. Every year on a certain day he used to hold a feast of exotic foods for all the people of the village so that he could prove that he was a man of charity. In turn he expected that all people who ate his food would pray for his health and happiness in this world as well as a place for him in Heaven.

Incidently, next day was the day of Malik Bhago's annual feast. Rich exotic foods were ready to be served. Special messengers were sent to bring every known holy man to the feast. When Malik Bhago heard the news that Nanak was also in the town, he felt very excited because who else could be more important to honour his feast and pray for him. He at once sent his messengers to ask Guru Nanak to come to his annual feast.

But Nanak declined the invitation. At this Malik Bhago was surprised as well as annoyed. His excitement changed into anger and he told his messengers to go back to Nanak and bring him to his house, by force if necessary.

This time, when the messengers came to fetch Nanak to Bhago's house, he did not refuse to accompany them. However, he took with him a piece of coarse 'ROTI' (Pancake-like bread), which Lalo had prepared for visitors.

In the meantime, a big crowd had already gathered outside Bhago's house to see what would happen to Guru Nanak when he reached there. Soon they saw Nanak. His face was radiant with a strange and penetrating smile. He seemed very happy to see such a large crowd. It was a good opportunity for him to teach his message.

As soon as Nanak entered the house, Malik Bhago spoke in an agitated manner and said, "Why is it that you have accepted coarse food from a low-caste carpenter, but do not wish to eat my richly-made dishes, which everybody else seems to enjoy so much?" Nanak did not answer, but asked for a THAALI * with food in it. This was brought immediately. Now Nanak sat down calmly. He gently picked a piece of richly greased 'POOREE' (a small fried pancake) from the Thaali *(large steel plate) in one hand and in the other he held a piece of roti brought from Lalo's house. He squeezed them both. To the amazement of everyone, drops of milk trickled out of Lalo's roti, and to the horror of Bhago drops of blood oozed out of his pooree .

Everybody present was stunned into silence, but Bhago shouted, "What trickery is this!" To this Nanak replied all the more politely, "No Bhago, no trickery, no magic, but the plain truth. Lalo's roti has come as a result of his honest labour. His roti is as pure as he is himself in his living, and so white milk symbolizes his truthful life. You, Malik Bhago, have not acquired your wealth by honest living. Your rich food is the result of the blood and sweat of many who work for you, and so this blook symbolizes your cruelty and tyranny".

It seemed that every word from the Guru shook Bhago to accept the truth. He could not deny what the Guru had said. His pride was instantly humbled and he felt a sudden change of mind. Without saying a single word he fell at the Guru's feet and begged for forgiveness. Guru Nanak lifted him up gently, embraced him and said, "Remember Bhago, your annual feast will bring you no credit until you really mean to help the poor and the weak. Charity given out of ill-earned wealth brings no blessings."

As he squeezed the two pieces, drops of blood came out from Malik Bhago's pooree and drops of milk trickled from Lalo's roti.

AT HARDWAR

During his Eastward journey NANAK wanted to visit a holy place of the Hindus, called HARDWAR. This little town is situated on the banks of the river GANGA (Ganges). The Ganga is regarded as the most holy river by the Hindus.

One morning, as he came to the river, he saw something strange and unusual. All along, the people were not only bathing but also throwing and offering water to the rising sun in the east.

It did not take him long to realise what was happening. But he too had a message: He quietly walked into the river near the bank and stood in the water with his back to the sun. Then he began to throw water in the opposite direction — to the west. This was unusual and strange for other people who were throwing water to the east.

Everybody bathing nearby looked at NANAK with amazement and surprise. Some thought he was mad or an insane person and took no notice, while others thought him ignorant and came near to tell him what was right. Soon there was a crowd, many watching and listening from the bank.

One wise looking man spoke to NANAK and asked him what he was doing. NANAK's technique had worked. He had got them into talking without asking the people to stop and listen to him. Immediately but politely he asked, "May I know what you are doing?". The man looked surprised at NANAK's question and said, "Don't you even know that? We are sending this water to our ancestors, now living in the other world, where the sun comes from."

At this, Guru NANAK smiled broadly, shook his head gently and again started to throw water in the opposite direction. Now everybody was getting impatient, because NANAK did not answer their questions, and did not stop doing something which they thought was wrong. The crowd on the bank was really big now.

The man spoke again. He seemed angry and annoyed at NANAK's behaviour. "But you have not explained to us. Why are you throwing water in the wrong direction?" Now NANAK was sure that everybody in the crowd was watching and listening. He said "I live in Panjab which is West of here. In Panjab I planted some crops before leaving. I have heard that there has been no rain since then. There is a drought. I am trying to save these crops from dying for lack of water. That is why I am throwing water to the west."

Most of the people in the crowd laughed at NANAK's reply without understanding the trap he had laid for them. The same person spoke to NANAK with even more scorn and anger. "Do you know your crops in Panjab are hundreds of miles away from here. How could this handful of water reach that far? Can't you see it actually falls a few feet away from where you are standing? Are you mad or just plain foolish?"

NANAK kept smiling all the time; and when the other man stopped his lecture, he began to speak very clearly but calmly. "I can see that this water is falling back into the GANGA a few feet away, but don't you see that the same thing is happening to the water which you throw towards the sun. If my water can't reach a few hundred miles away in Panjab, then how can you pretend that the water which you throw to provide for your ancestors land would reach millions of miles further away than my land?"

Everybody in the crowd was stunned to hear this argument. But soon there were whispers. Suddenly they realised that this man was not an ordinary man. They were repentant. They asked him to tell them something more. NANAK in turn told them not to waste time in rituals which served no purpose, which did not do any good to others, and which they did not even understand. His explanation was complete and so was his message.

GURU NANAK AT HARDWAR

First, they laughed at him and told him that he was wrong, but then they listened and realised their own mistake.

AT MECCA (MAKKAH)

Nanak loved both Hindus and Muslims as his friends. However, he always claimed that he was neither a Hindu nor a Muslim but the child of God. At the same time, he did not miss visiting the holy places of the Hindus and Muslims alike. He used these visits to meet more people and teach them the truth.

One of his journeys took him to Mecca which is over two thousand miles to the west of Panjab in Saudi Arabia. This was the time of HAJJ, when Muslim pilgrims pay their respects to their Prophet Mohammed by visiting the holy shrine, KAABA in Mecca.

The journey had taken months. Most of the time Nanak either rode a camel or walked on foot. The night he reached Mecca he was very tired. He lay down for a rest and sleep in the holy precinct round the shrine. When he was fast asleep he was suddenly woken up by a rude shout and a kick from an angry Hajji-pilgrim. "What is the matter? O man of God, why are you so angry?" Nanak inquired.

"Don't you see that you are sleeping with your legs stretched towards the Kaaba, the House of God?" the man shouted again.

"I am sorry, I did not mean disrespect to the house of God. I am his child too. But, brother, would you please turn my feet to the direction where God is not."

It is said that as this man turned Nanak's feet in another direction, to his amazement he realised that they were still facing the Kaaba. The man was totally confused. In the meantime the Guru stood up and blessed the man for tolerance and understanding.

"Mehar masit sidak musalla haq halal Koran"

Make thy mosque of love of humanity;
Thy prayer-carpet of sincerity;
Thy Koran of honest and approved endeavour;
Thy circumcision of modesty;
Thy Ramadan fast of noble conduct—
Thus shalt thou be a true Muslim.
Make good deeds thy Kaaba;
Truthfulness thy preceptor;
Thy Namaz and Kalima pure actions;

Five are the prayers, five the hours to perform;
Five their different names;
What are the true prayers?
The first is truthfulness; the next honest endeavour;
The third, prayer offered to God for good of all;
The fourth is a sincere heart;
The fifth, devotion to God:
Whose Kalima is good actions is alone a true Muslim.
Saith Nanak: All who are false within,
Prove of no worth in the end.

(Var Majh, Guru Nanak, The Holy Granth — P.140)

"Musalman kahawan mushkal"

Hard it is to become a true Muslim;
Only one truly such may be so called.
His first action, to love the way of the holy;
Second, to shed off his heart's filth as on the grindstone.
One professing to be a guide to Muslims must shed the
illusions of life and death.
To God's Will must he submit;
Obey God and efface his self.
Such a one shall be a blessing for all,
And be truly reckoned a Muslim.

(Var Majh, Guru Nanak, p.141)

GURU NANAK AT MAKKAH

"Please turn my feet in a direction in which God is not"

THE DEPARTURE

Guru Nanak's life story is full of mysteries.

There are many stories and incidents related to Guru Nanak which look so strange and unbelievable today, but which actually happened and were witnessed by people present at the time. The departure of Guru Nanak from this mortal world was no less a mystery.

It is said that Guru Nanak knew that his time to leave for his heavenly abode was approaching. So he had the task of choosing his successor who could continue his message of truth, equality and love. He had two sons. Nanak did not choose either.

One claimed to be a good man living the life of an ascetic in the forest.

"What does he know about the real world, and the joys and sorrows of family life? What does he know about fighting sin when he has not ever faced sin? How could he preach or teach people when he does not live among people?" These were some of the Guru's questions when someone suggested his son's name.

The second son was married, but he was too much absorbed in the business he owned and was more interested in making money than in serving people. He too claimed GURGADDI (Guru's place). Thus both the sons were unfit to carry on with the task of leading his followers after he had departed.

In the meantime the Guru had devised some tests for his followers, and among them he had chosen one. Nobody knew beforehand that they were being tested, and everybody was surprised when Guru Nanak declared that a Sikh (follower) named LENHA was his choice. He then renamed him as "ANGAD" meaning 'of my own body.'

Now that Guru Nanak had named his successor and he was satisfied that his message would be carried forward by his most capable Sikh, Guru Angad, he prepared himself for his last journey to rejoin his Master.

The next morning, the followers found that the Guru's soul had departed, leaving his body behind. Soon, as the word spread, people began to flock to the Guru's house. There were both Hindus and Muslims which the Guru had loved and taught. They were his followers who had great respect and love for the Guru. But within hours of the departure of the Guru both Hindus and Muslims were arguing with each other. The Hindus wanted to cremate the body while the Muslims were insistent that it should be buried. Both had forgotton that the Guru had said 'I am neither Hindu, nor Muslim but the child of God, and a servant of the whole human race.' Both had forgotton one of the Guru's teachings 'not to do anything for the sake of a ritual and without understanding it.' Thus the people had yet much to learn.

As the story goes, there came an old man who stopped the two groups arguing with each other. He made a suggestion which both accepted readily. The suggestion was, 'let the Hindus go and bring fresh flowers to be placed beside the Guru's body on one side, and similarly let the Muslims go and bring fresh flowers which will be placed on the other side of the Guru's body. Then both should wait for morning — and the people whose flowers remain fresh shall claim the body."

Both Hindus and Muslims followed the instructions of this wise old man. Next morning, to the surprise of everyone, both the bunches of flowers were as fresh as ever. But there was no 'body' underneath the Kaffan (white sheet covering). Now the same man appeared again and told the two groups of followers to divide the 'white sheet' and dispose of it according to their wishes. They quickly agreed.

Thus the Hindus burned their piece of cloth and the Muslims buried their part. Later, both wanted to build a small monument in memory of the Guru. Again they were divided and built two different ones on the outskirts of the village near RAVI. But they were soon reminded that the Guru did not wish divisions between Hindus and Muslims. The River Ravi burst its banks and both buildings were lost.

GURU NANAK'S 'DEPARTURE'

They brought fresh flowers and placed them on each side of the Guru's body.

GLOSSARY OF SIKH TERMS

(In conceptual order)

SIKH:
(literally the word Sikh means a student or a learner) A Sikh is a member of a religious order founded by Guru Nanak in the 15th century. He is a believer of one God and a keeper of 'His Image'.

To say that SIKHISM is a branch of Hinduism is as much correct or incorrect as to say that Christianity is a branch of Judaism.

GURU:
(literally the word guru means a teacher) More common meaning of the guru is, a spiritual leader, a saint, a maharishi, a yogi or a swami.

However, the meaning of the word Guru in Sikh terminology is at a further higher level, and it stands for the 'prophet'.

WAHEGURU:
(literally, the wonderful teacher) To Sikhs 'Waheguru' stands for the God, the Lord, the Creator.

GURDWARA:
(literally, Guru's door/place) A Gurdwara is a place of worship of the Sikhs. The use of word 'temple' or 'Sikhs temple' for a Gurdwara is as much correct or incorrect as to call a church a Christian temple, or a temple as a Hindu church.

GURPURB:
Guru's remembrance day — the birth or death. May be treated as a holy day and holiday.

GURU-GRANTH:
(lit. Granth means a large book) It is also called the ADI-GRANTH; 'adi' means the original first. The holy Guru Granth is not only the scriptures of the Sikh, it is regarded as the living 'body' (voice) of the Gurus, and thus accorded an extreme respect worthy of a prophet.

GURBANI:
The uttered 'WORD' or verses of the Gurus compiled in the holy Granth.

GURMUKHI:
The visible form of Gurbani as seen written in the holy Granth.

GRANTHI:
The professional reader of the Guru Granth.

KHALSA:
(lit. 'Khalsa' means pure) The Sikh brotherhood.

KHANDA:
The emblem of the Sikh nation ( ) named after the double-edged sword in the middle.

SINGH:
(literally means lion) Suffix for all male Sikh names e.g. Ranjit Singh, Parminder Singh. Can be followed by family name i.e. Ranjit Singh Gill, Parminder Singh Bajwa.

KAUR:
(literally means princess) Suffix for all female Sikh names e.g. Ranjit Kaur, Parminder Kaur. Can be followed by family name e.g. Ranjit Kaur Gill.

AMRIT:
(literally means the elixir of life) The holy water for the baptising ceremony; the nectar.

AMRITSAR:
(lit. sar or srovar means the pool or the tank — thus the pool of nectar or elixir) Amritsar is the name of the holy city of the Sikhs, named after the holy pool in the middle of the Golden Temple complex.

ARDAS: The prayer — or the act of praying with palms together.

PARSHAD: (lit. food) The holy symbolic food (sweet) served after the conclusion of Sikh service and Ardas. Also called 'Karrah-parshad'.

LANGAR: The kitchen — which serves free food to all people irrespective of their caste, creed, colour or status. Where there is a Gurdwara, there is a LANGAR.

SHABAD: (lit. means word) The 'revealed word' uttered by the Guru; a hymn or a verse from the Holy Granth.

KEERTAN: The reciting or singing of the 'Shabad' with the help of musical instruments e.g. Baja and Tabla.

RAAGI: The professional singer of the holy word or the 'shabad'.

DHADHI: The professional ballad singer and narrator of Sikh history.

BAISAKHI: The new year and the harvest festival of Panjab. Also an important Sikh festival marking the birth of the KHALSA.

BHANGRA: The popular folk dance of the people of Panjab, usually associated with Baisakhi.

KESH: Long hair. Sikhs keep long hair as a symbol of humility and an acceptance of God's Will.

KANGHA: A special small wooden comb, also symbolic of cleanliness and care.

KARRA: The steel bangle which is symbolic of strength and unity, and a bond with the Guru and the Sikh brotherhood.

KACHHA: A special type of pair of shorts or underpants.

KIRPAAN: The kirpaan (Sikh sword) is symbolic of respect, justice and authority. A small 6" kirpaan which a Sikh wears must not be referred to as a dagger or knife.

PANJ PIAREY: (lit. the five beloved ones; the original members of the Khalsa) Nowadays a body of any five baptised or fully practising Sikhs (male or female) is regarded as capable of taking decisions and making judgements on most Sikh matters.

PANTH: The organised body of Sikhs — the 'Khalsa Panth'.

SANGAT: The congregation in a Gurdwara.

PANGAT: A special seating arrangement or principle of sharing communal food in Langar.

SABHA: Lit. a society or an association; 'Singh Sabha' means Sikh Organisation.

ANAND-KAARJ: Sikh religious marriage ceremony.

AKHAND-PATTH: A special non-stop reading of the holy Granth by professional readers taking almost 48 hours.

Selected Book List on SIKHISM and SIKH HISTORY

A select Bibliography of the Sikhs and Sikhism	Ganda Singh
Private Correspondence Anglo Sikh Wars	" "
A History of the Sikhs (Vo. 1 & 2)	Khushwant Singh
The Spirit Born People	Puran Singh
The Sikh Religion (3 Vols.)	M.A. Macauliffe
Guru Nanak & the Origin of Sikh Faith	Harbans Singh
The Heritage of the Sikhs	" "
Guru Nanak & the Sikh Religion	W.H. McLeod
Guru Nanak, Apostle of Love	G.S. Mansukhani
Travels of Guru Nanak	Panjab University, Chandigarh
Guru Gobind Singh	S.S. Johar
Guru Gobind, the Saint Warrior	Parkash Singh
The Granth of Guru Gobind Singh	C.H. Loehlin
Jallianwala Bagh	Panjab University, Chandigarh
Universal Sikhism	A.S. Sethi
Sikhism	Taja Singh
The Sikh Religion	" "
Essays on Sikhism	" "
The Sikhs of Panjab	W.H. McLeod
History of the Sikhs	J.D. Cunnungham
Social & Political Philosophy of Guru Gobind	Sher Singh
The Sikhs	W. Owen Cole
Encyclopedia of Sikh History and Religion (3 Vols.)	P.S. Gill
Guru Nanak	Tarlochan Singh
Rise of Sikh Power and Maharaja Ranjit Singh	S.S. Seetal
Transformation of Sikhism	Sir G.C. Narang
Evolution of the KHALSA	I.B. Banerjee
History of the Panjab	Mohamed Laliff
Philosophy of Sikhism	Sher Singh
Glimpses of the Divine Masters	Ranbir Singh
The Baisakhi of Guru Gobind Singh	Kapur Singh
GURU GRANTH SAHIB (Eng. Translation 8 Vols.)	Manmohan Singh
The Gospel of the Guru Granth Sahib	Duncan Greenless
Sri Guru GRANTH SAHIB in 4 Vols.	Gopal Singh
A Critical Study of Adi Granth	S.S. Kohli
Sacred Writings of the Sikhs	UNESCO (Tarlochan Singh)
The Guru in Sikhism	W. Owen Cole
The Sikhs Today	Khushwant Singh
Sikh Sacred Music	S.S.M. Society
Sikh Studies Part 1 & 2	Sikh Advisory Board, Singapore
Stories from Sikh History Vol. 1 to 8	Dhillon & Singh (Hemkunt Press)
The Story of Guru Nanak stories for children	Mala Singh
Guru Nanak	Daljit Singh
History and Philosophy of Sikhism	Khazan Singh
Guru Nanak Re-interpreted	Narain Singh
The Sikhs of the Panjab	R.E. Parry
A Short History of the Sikhs	C.H. Payne
Religious and Short History of the Sikhs	G.B. Scott

SOME RECENT BOOKS ON THE PANJAB CRISIS

Tragedy of Panjab:

Operation Blue Star and After	Kushwant Singh and Kuldip Nayer
The Siege Within	M.J. Akbar
Bhindranwale: Myth and Reality	Chand Joshi
Happenings in Panjab	Harkishan S. Surjit
The Panjab Story	Amarjit, A. Shorie, J.S. Arora, Kushwant Singh
The Invasion of the Golden Temple	Dr. S.S. Kapoor
The Assassination and After	S. Gupta A. Shorie, R. Bedi, P. Roy
Amritsar — Mrs. Gandhi's Last Battle	Mark Tully and Satish Jacob
Oppression in Panjab	Rao, Ghose, Bhattacharya, Ahuja, Pancholi (A Hind Mazdoor Kisan Publication)
Who are Guilty?	People's Union for Democratic Rights & People's Union for Civil Liberties

SOME MAGAZINES AND NEWSPAPERS

The Sikh Courier — Quarterly	88 Mollison Way, Edgware, London HA8 5QW Tel: 01-592 1215
The Sikh Messenger — Quarterly	43 Dorset Road, Merton Park, London SW19 3EZ Tel: 01-540 4148
The Sikh Review — Monthly	116 Karnani Mansion, Park Street, Calcutta 700 016, INDIA
Journal of Sikh Studies	The Registrar, Guru Nanak Dev University, Amritsar 143 001, PANJAB, INDIA
The Spokesman — Weekly	6 Northend Complex, R.K. Ashram Marg, New Delhi 110 001, INDIA

SOME USEFUL ADDRESSES FOR THE BOOKS LISTED

Independent Publishing Company	38 Kennington Lane, London, SE11 4LS Tel: 01-735 2101
Books from India (U.K.) Ltd.	45 Museum Street, London WC1 Tel: 01-405 7226
Star Books International	112 Whitefield Street, London WC1 Tel: 01-388 9832/387-0610
Singh Brothers	Bazar Mai Sewa, Amritsar, Panjab, INDIA
New Book Company	Mai Hiran Gate, Jalandhar, Panjab, INDIA
Hemkunt Press	A-78 Naraina Industrial Area, Phase I, New Delhi, INDIA
The Sikh Education Council U.K.	10 Featherstone Road, Southall, Middlesex, England Tel: 01-574 1902

Appendix

REHAT MARYADA

The Rehat Maryada is the most comprehensive and respected document drawn up under the auspices of the SHIROMANI GURDWARA PARBANDHAK COMMITTEE (the Supreme Religious Parliament of Sikhs, constituted under the Sikh Gurdwaras Act, 1925) by a dedicated group of renowned Sikh scholars and priests summarising the instructions of the ten Gurus and outlining the Sikh way of life in consultation with REHAT NAMAAS of the learned Sikhs and writers of the period.

The first meeting of the Religious Advisory Sub-committee was held on 4.5.1931 at the AKAL TAKHAT, and after many more meetings and consultations, alterations and amendments to the drafts in the subsequent years, the document was finally approved by the S.G.P.C. on 3.2.1945.

Some extracts from the Rehat Maryada (English version released on 20.11.1978 by the SGPC) are given here for the interest of readers and researchers.

AMRIT OR SIKH BAPTISM

(a)   The *Amrit* ceremony is held in some place which must not be a thoroughfare.

(b)   The Holy Guru Granth Sahib is opened. One Sikh is required to sit before it, and five others to conduct the ceremony. These are called *Panj Pyaras,* or the Five Beloved Ones. Women are also eligible for the work. All these Sikhs should wash themselves and their hair, and should be wearing all the five symbols called the Five K's *Kesh* (long hair), *Kangha* (comb), *Kachh* (knickers), *Kara* (iron bracelet) and *Kirpaan* (sword).

(c)   None of the Five Beloved Ones should be blind, half-blind, or disabled. None should have committed a breach of the baptismal vows. All should be fit in every way: strong, healthy, cheerful, and tidy.

(d)   The Sikh baptism is open to men and women of all countries, of whatever race, creed, or caste. The recipients must not be too young. They should wash their hair, and should have the five K's on their person, and no mark or symbol of any other religion. They should not have their heads bare or covered with a cap or hat. No earings are allowed. The wearing of other ornaments is also discouraged. All should stand reverently with folded hands.

(e)   If any one has to be rebaptized on account of some breach of the rules, he is taken to one side by the Five and some penalty is imposed upon him, after which he is allowed to rejoin the rest.

(f)   The party is then addressed by one of the Five who explains the principles of Sikhism, including belief in the Oneness of God, His love as the only way of salvation, practice of the Name and the Guru's Word as the means of awakening that love in one's heart, and service of all with selflessness and sacrifice.

(g)   They are asked whether they accept these principles. When they give their assent, one of the Five offers prayer for the preparation of *Amrit:* and the person sitting before the Holy Guru Granth Sahib reads out a Hukam from it. Then all the Five begin to prepare the *Amrit,* or the water of immortality.

(h)   They place an iron vessel on a pedestal and, sitting round it, put water and a suitable quantity of sweets *(patashahs)* into it. They sit in what is called the 'heroic attitude' with the left knee up and the right knee on the ground.

(i)   They recite the following five selected compositions of Gurbani in a loud voice:
The *Japji, Jap,* Ten *Swayas, Chaupai* from *Dasam Granth* and 6 stanzas from the *Anand.*
The reciter, looking intently into the water and placing his left hand on the edge of the vessel, continues stirring the water with a double-edged sword *(Khanda)* which he holds in his right hand. The rest keep both their hands on the vessel, and their eyes fixed on the water.

(j)   When the recitation is over, all the Five stand up with the vessel in their hands, and one of them offers prayer. The Amrit is now ready.

(k)   Each candidate is called up and told to seat himself or herself in the 'heroic attitude' (Bir Asan) described above. S/he is asked to make a cup of his/her hands, by placing the right hand over the left, and to receive five handfuls of the Amrit one after another. As each handful is drunk by the recipient, the giver of the Amrit shouts *"Waheguru Ji Ka Khalsa, Waheguru Ji Ki Fateh",* and the recipient repeats it after him. Then his or her eyes and hair are touched with the Amrit five times; each time the recipient is asked to repeat the above words after the giver of the Amrit. What is left is drunk off, turn by turn, by all the candidates, sipping directly from the vessel. Thus, they become 'Brothers or Sisters of the Golden Cup'.

(l) Then the Five initiators with one voice utter the following invocation to God, given in the beginning of the *Japji,* and the initiated persons repeat it after them:

"God, the one Supreme Being, of the True Name, the Creater, without Fear and Enmity, Immortal, Unborn, Self-existent, and the Enlightener; can be realized through Guru's grace".

This is done five times.

(m) One of the Five then administers the *Rehat,* or the vows of Sikh discipline.

He tells them that they are to consider themselves as children of the same parents. Their father is Guru Gobind Singh and their mother is Mata Sahib Kaur. Their home is Keshgarh. All the differences based on their previous religions, castes and occupations are done away with, and they begin afresh as the 'purified ones', as the Khalsa who believe in one God and in no other gods or goddesses; who conduct themselves by the teachings of the Ten Gurus and put their faith in no other guide or book. They are to offer the daily prayers regularly, pay tithes, and are never to part with any of the five K's. They are to abstain from the following four main taboos, called Kuraihts: (1) Removal of hair, (2) Eating meat cut and prepared in Muslim fashion *(Halal),* (3) Adultery and (4) Using tobacco in any form.

(n) If a Sikh commits any of these breaches of discipline, he becomes a *'patit'* (apostate) and has to get himself rebaptized.

The following are some of the minor taboos, called *'tankhan':*

(1) Entering into brotherhood with any of the recalcitrant Sikhs, like the *Minas, Masands, Dhirmalias,* and *Ram Raias* or with those who, having once accepted Sikhism, take to shaving, smoking, or committing infanticide.

(2) Dining from the same dish with a person unbaptised or an apostate.

(3) Dyeing or picking out any white hair.

(4) Receiving money in return for a daughter's hand in marriage. (The same taboo now extends to a bribe received on a son's marriage).

(5) Using any narcotic drug or intoxicant (opium, wine, poppy, hemp, cocaine etc.).

(6) Performing any ceremony which violates any of the Sikh Principles.

(7) The breaking of any vow taken at Amrit (baptism) ceremony.

(n) After this, one of the five offers prayer, and the person sitting before Holy Guru Granth Sahib reads out a passage.

(o) Those who are new to Sikhism must be renamed. The new name is given to them in the manner already described under the naming ceremony.

(p) At the end *Karah Prasad* is distributed. All the newly initiated Sikhs eat *Karah Prasad* out of the same vessel.

DISCIPLINE OF ORGANIZATION

(a) **Guru Panth**:- All Amrit-Dhari (baptized) Sikhs acting together with the sense of Guru in them constitute the *Guru Panth.*

(b) **Gur Sangat**:- Wherever there are at least five regular Sikhs, they can form a Sangat. When they act in a representative capacity with the sense of the Guru in them, they constitute a *Guru Sangat* . The Presence of Guru Granth Sahib in their midst is essential.

(c) **Panthic Meeting**:- Such units meeting as a whole (as was the custom in the early days when the numbers were small) or through their accredited representatives (as is done nowadays) form a meeting of the *Panth.*

(d) **Gurmattas**:- All decisions affecting the whole community are made by such a panthic meeting. These decisions are called *Gurmattas.*

(e) For a *Gurmatta* only those subjects can be taken up which are calculated to clarify and support the fundamental principles of Sikhism; such as safeguarding the position of the Gurus and the Holy Guru Granth Sahib, purity of the ritual and the Panthic organization. On other questions such as political, social or educational matters, only a *matta* or resolution can be passed, which is not as sacred and **inviolable** as a *Gurmatta.*

(f) The appeal against the decision of local *Sangats* lies with the *Akal Takhat,* but the decisions of the Panth are inviolable and are binding on all Sikhs.

(g) These decisions are conveyed to the Sangat in the form of *Hukamnamas,* or orders issued from the *Akal Takht.*

(h) All cases of reference about the rituals are disposed of by the *Akal Takhat.* These decisions are also proclaimed in the form of *Hukamnamas.*

SEWA (SERVICE)

Service is an essential part of a Sikh's duty. It is the practical expression of love. Those whom one is to serve must be loved. The caste system and its accompanying evil of untouchability have, therefore, no place in a religion of service. Service recognizes no barriers of religion, caste, or race. It must be offered to all; it should not take the fixed forms of sectarian charity, but should be freely varied according to the reasonable needs of those whom we want to help.

Gurdwaras are the laboratories for teaching the practice of service, for which the real field is the world abroad. The service in Gurdwaras takes the form of sweeping the floor, cleaning utensils, fetching water, and pulling or waving the *pankhas* or fans, but the most important institution in this connection is the Guru's Free Kitchen.

LANGAR (FREE KITCHEN)

(a)   The institution of *Guru Ka Langar* or Free Kitchen, is as old as Sikhism. It was started by Guru Nanak for the purpose of teaching service, spreading equality, and removing untouchability and other prejudices born of the caste system.

(b)   In a way, the kitchen in all Sikh homes is *Guru Ka Langar,* as they are enjoined to share their food with others. They are also expected to take part in the running of the common free kitchens opened at Gurdwaras. They may contribute provisions, pay for the expenses, or personally lend a hand in cleaning utensils, fetching water or fuel, or in the cooking and distribution of food.

(c)   Non-Sikhs are also freely allowed to help in the maintenance of the kitchen.

(d)   No invidious distinction is to be made between person and person, between a Sikh and a non-Sikh, between a 'poor' and a 'rich', when making seating arrangements or serving food in the Guru's Kitchen.

AKHAND PATH (Non-stop Reading of the Holy Guru Granth Sahib)

(Non-stop Reading of the Holy Guru Granth Sahib)

(a)   *Akhand Path* is done to mark special occasions of great joy, sorrow or distress. The complete reading (carried out by a number of people in a series of shifts) takes approximately 48 hours. The reading must be clear and accurate and not too fast, so that it can be easily understood.

(b)   Any person who asks for or arranges *Akhand Path* should, as far as possible, ensure that the reading is done by himself, his family or friends. If, for any reason, such a person is unable to get such help in the reading, he should at least listen to as much of the reading as possible. It is wrong for people to arrange for *Akhand Path* without their being prepared to either read or listen to it. Those asked to help in the reading may be given food and sustenance, according to the means of those that arrange the *Path.*

(c)   No other book should be read while *Path* is going on, nor is the presence of *JOTE* or *KUMBH* advisable.

(d)   Before starting *Akhand Path,* the first five verses and the last verse of the *Anand Sahib* should be read, followed by the *Ardas* and *Hukum.* This should be followed by the distribution of *Karah Prasad* (Holy Communion) to the congregation. Then the *Akhand Path* can be commenced.

(e)   A complete reading (either continuous or non-continuous) of the Holy Guru Granth Sahib should be followed by a reading of the *Mundawni.* The *Ragmala* may or may not be recited according to the local custom or according to the wishes of the person or persons who arrange such a Reading (Path). The *Anand Mundawni* is then read and followed by the *Ardas* and *Hukum.* After *Akhand Path, Karah Prasad* is distributed to the congregation.

(f)   At the time of the *Akhand Path* it is usual to give donations for the upkeep of the Gurdwara and for the furtherance of Sikhism. This should be given according to one's means.

TAKHATS (Thrones of Panthic authority) A Takhat is a Gurdwara of extra-ordinatory historical and religious importance.

There are five — i)   The Akal Takhat Sahib in Amritsar
                 ii) Sri Keshgarh Sahib at Anandpur
                 iii) Sri Patna Sahib at Patna
                 iv) Sri Damdama Sahib at Talwandi Sabo
                 v)   Sri Hazoor Sahib at Nander.

N.B. Only AMRITDHARI Sikhs, who observe the baptismal vows, are allowed to enter the innermost part of a Takhat; all other parts of the Takhat are open to everybody.